PRINT'S BEST LETTERHEADS & BUSINESS CARDS 4

PRINT'S BEST LETTERHEADS & BUSINESS CARDS 4

Library of Congress Catalog Card Number 89-091067
ISBN 1-883915-01-5

RC PUBLICATIONS

President and Publisher: Howard Cadel
Vice President and Editor: Martin Fox
Creative Director: Andrew Kner
Managing Director, Book Projects: Linda Silver
Administrative Assistant: Nancy Silver
Assistant Art Director: Michele L. Trombley

Steven Heller, who wrote the
introduction to this volume, is
art director of the New York
Times Book Review, editor of
the AIGA Journal, and a
contributing editor to PRINT
magazine.

Print's Best
LETTERHEADS & BUSINESS CARDS 4

WINNING DESIGNS FROM PRINT MAGAZINE'S NATIONAL COMPETITION

Edited by
LINDA SILVER

Introduction by
STEVEN HELLER

Designed by
ANDREW KNER

Published by
RC PUBLICATIONS, INC.
NEW YORK, NY

A letterhead and business card tell more about the way a business or individual wants to be publicly recognized than any other form of graphic communication. These are at once brands, like those burned into cattle hides; banners, like those carried into battle; and signs, like those that provide directions. The design of these materials may often appear simple, but in fact, they are among the most charged, and therefore among the most difficult, problems a graphic designer must solve.

Just ask any designer how long it took to design his own letterhead/business card combination. He'll probably say it seemed like ages. Deciding on the perfect typeface, determining the best image, and specifying the right colors can be as difficult as naming the business itself, and they usually must last as long. No wonder designers' clients are often equally indecisive when having to choose in what manner they will be graphically represented. Unlike many design decisions, selecting the letterhead/business card, even one based on an existing logo, does not depend on research, analysis, and other (pseudo) scientific methods, but rather on instinct; as in how well will that cute drawing in the left-hand corner signal who and what is being represented? Or will a minimal line of sans-serif type or a bolder slab serif be the best evocation of a particular business persona?

As the offspring of intuition, the letterhead/business card can be as much a work of art as a corporate system. And yet both letterhead and business card are governed by various restrictions, not the least of which are size and shape. Conventional standards imposed by what the post office and a billfold (or briefcase compartment) will bear force the letterhead/business card into a few monotonous forms. However, within these constraints there are numerous possibilities for creative maneuvering. Judging from this volume, there is certainly enough good work being

CONTENTS

done in letterhead/business card design to fill a substantial-sized book. And as this particular sampling attests, the letterhead/business card (and let's not forget that often ignored vessel, the envelope) are *tabulas rasa* on which a wealth of backgrounds, foregrounds, pictures, symbols, silhouettes, and letterforms appear.

An overwhelming majority of these letterhead/business cards are designed for suppliers of creative services: graphic designers, copywriters, illustrators, photographers, etc. One can expect no less than exemplary graphics from these people, such as the clever way that illustrator Dave LaFleur shows off his drawing abilities by under-printing various light sketches on his letter and envelope (page 10), or the three narrative Old West images — in each a pencil is the primary symbol — that run through copywriter Patrick Jennings stationery and cards (page 23). But among these jewels are also a fair number of witty, elegant, and otherwise inspired designs for non-designers, among them a chiropractor whose letterhead reads "Dr. Greg Dahl (See back for details)" while the verso shows a classical anatomical illustration indicating various physical discomforts (page 24); a building contractor whose logo is the evolution of a classically modern structure (page 50); a mystery writer whose letterhead and envelope feature embossed pieces of a puzzle (page 53); and an auto technician whose fingerprint stains frame his stationery and card (page 67).

Unlike most other ephemeral graphic design, the letterhead/business card (as well as the envelope and billhead) are designed to withstand the vagaries of fashion and be used continually for an indefinite period of time. Of course, a letterhead can be changed as often as one's budget allows, but the best ones — those that evoke a strong identity — can last forever, or at least until the initial print run is thoroughly used up.—*Steven Heller*

5

P.O. Box #781714
Wichita, KS 67278
Tel 316 942 2424
Fax 316 942 8927

P.O. Box #781714
Wichita, KS 67278
Tel 316 685 3955
Fax 316 687 9477

EXPERIMENT ONE

JAKE'S EASY TO BUILD ELECTRIC MOTOR

DESCRIPTION: In three or four minutes, you can construct a very simple electric motor.

YOU WILL NEED: A thick rubber band, two paper clips, a 1.5 volt "D" cell, a small disc-shaped magnet, a few inches of wire (#22 gauge, non-insulated, varnish coated wire works well. It can be obtained at a radio or hardware store.).

HERE'S HOW:

1. To make the rotating part of the motor (the field coil), coil ten turns of the #22 wire, leaving a slight hook on the long ends, as shown in the illustration.

2. Scrape the varnish off of the top half of the two wire ends.

3. As shown, use the two paper clips to form supports for the coil.

4. Use the rubber band to hold the coil supports at the ends of the D cell.

5. Secure the magnet with tape or glue to the middle of the cell.

6. Place the coil into the supports and give the coil a gentle "flick."

The coil will rotate — you have built an electric motor.

WHAT'S HAPPENING: An electric current flows from one end of the cell, through the paper clip support and the coil, to the other end of the cell. As the current flows through the coil it creates a magnetic field in the coil, which is pushed by the field of the magnet on the side of the cell. The current flows as the bare side of the coil wire comes in contact with the paper clips. The varnish on the other side of the wire does not allow the current to flow. The on-off cycle of the current allows the coil to rotate.

THE CHALLENGE: Can you find other items around the house that can be used as parts of your electric motor?

EXPERIMENT 2

SEWER LEECHES

DESCRIPTION: With a little knowledge of science, you can make a colony of imaginary creatures that will amaze and fool your friends.

YOU WILL NEED: A tall, narrow glass container, clear, carbonated soft drink or club soda, a few raisins, and a dark piece of cloth.

HERE'S HOW:

1. Wash and rinse the glass thoroughly.

2. Slowly fill the glass with the soft drink. Try to avoid making foam.

3. Carefully drop in a few raisins.

4. At first, the raisins will sink. Eventually, they will "swim" to the surface and return to the bottom of the cylinder. They will repeat the cycle for several minutes.

5. Cover the glass with the cloth. Remove it when you show your colony of sewer leeches to your friends.

THE CHALLENGE: Can you find other items around the house that can be used as parts of your electric motor?

WHAT'S HAPPENING: The soft drink contains a gas called carbon dioxide, or CO_2. Bubbles of the gas collect on the sides of the raisins. Eventually, there will be enough bubbles on the raisins to make it float to the surface. Some of the bubbles will break at the surface and the raisin will sink to the bottom. From a distance, the raisins actually look like small creatures swimming in the liquid.

THE CHALLENGE: Develop as many explanations as you can about your imaginary creatures.

WHERE DID YOU CAPTURE THEM? WHAT DO YOU FEED THEM? WHY DON'T THEY LIKE THE LIGHT?

You might be able to fool your friends for only a few minutes, but it is some good science fun to try!

FACTOIDS

The **RED SKY** seen at sunrise and sunset is caused by the scattering of light. Sunlight is a mixture of many different colors of light. The short waves of blue light are scattered by dust particles in the air. Red light has a longer wavelength and is able to pass through the dusty air.

The white halo sometimes seen around the **MOON** is caused by tiny ice crystals in the upper atmosphere.

The average **RAINBOW** lasts about 7 minutes.

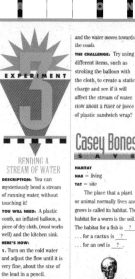

Backyard ZOO

PRAYING MANTIS: The praying mantis is one of the few insects that is valued by man. It is valuable because it eats many other harmful insects.

The mantis gets its name from the position of its front legs. The legs are equipped with spikes used to hold its food. The mantis has very powerful jaws, but is harmless to humans.

HOUSING THE PRAYING MANTIS: You can keep the mantis in a large jar with holes punched in the lid, or a small aquarium with a screen over the top. The mantis needs room to move around.

Place sand or soil in the bottom of the jar. Provide some branches for climbing. Include a shallow dish or jar lid with water and a stone to hold it in place. You may need to place the jar near a 25w light bulb to provide heat. Try to maintain the same temperature and humidity as the location where you found the mantis. The mantis will not survive cold temperatures.

DIET: The mantis will eat live crickets and other small insects. They will even capture houseflies.

Element OF THE MONTH

CARBON What do diamonds, pencil lead and charcoal have in common? They are all made of carbon. Carbon reacts so easily with other elements that over 1 million carbon compounds are known to exist, such as carbon dioxide, gasoline, nylon, sugar, cellulose (paper), and natural gas.

EXPERIMENT 3

BENDING A STREAM OF WATER

DESCRIPTION: You can mysteriously bend a stream of running water, without touching it!

YOU WILL NEED: A plastic comb, an inflated balloon, a piece of dry cloth, (wool works well) and the kitchen sink.

HERE'S HOW:

1. Turn on the cold water and adjust the flow until it is very fine, about the size of the lead in a pencil.

2. Brush your hair with the plastic comb and bring the comb near the stream of water. Do not touch the water with the comb.

3. The stream of water will bend towards the comb.

WHAT'S HAPPENING: Pulling the comb through your hair creates a charge of static electricity on the comb. The field created around the comb causes an opposite charge to be created in the stream of water. The opposite charges are attracted to each other and the water moves towards the comb.

THE CHALLENGE: Try using different items, such as stroking the balloon with the cloth, to create a static charge and see if it will affect the stream of water. How about a ruler or piece of plastic sandwich wrap?

Casey Bones SAYS

HABITAT

HAB = living
TAT = site

The place that a plant or animal normally lives and grows is called its habitat. The habitat for a worm is the soil.

The habitat for a fish is ___?
... for a cactus is ___?
... for an owl is ___?

Cover (left) and spread (above) from newsletter that was part of promotion.

Promotional stationery for a children's television science show.

DESIGN FIRM: Gardner + Greteman, Wichita, Kansas

ART DIRECTORS/ DESIGNERS: Sonia Greteman, Bill Gardner

MAC ARTIST: Karen Hogan

BUDGET: Design: $2500; printing: $2500

PRINTING PROCESS: 4-color

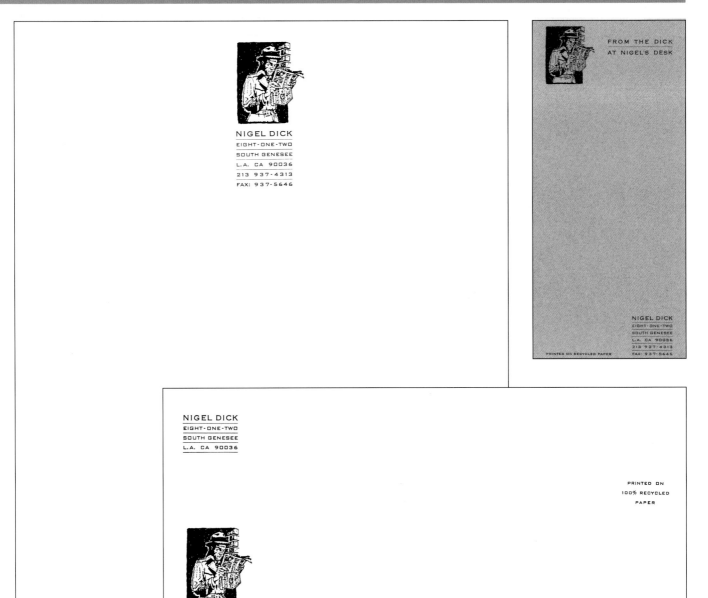

Personal and business stationery. Part of a long-running series including "Once a Dick, Always a Dick"; "Spot the Dick"; "Private Dick." The image was an engraving of a cleaned up rubber stamp.

DESIGN FIRM: Zida Borcich Letterpress, Fort Bragg, California

ART DIRECTORS: Zida Borcich, Nigel Dick

DESIGNER: Zida Borcich

PRINTING PROCESS: Letterpress—hand-set lead type and magnesium engraving of Private Dick.

Stationery establishes a fresh identity that emphasizes the personal involvement of the two owners in the creative process.

DESIGN FIRM:

Simon & Cirulis, Inc.,

St. Louis, Missouri

CREATIVE DIRECTOR:

Mike Simon

ART DIRECTOR/

DESIGNER: Maris Cirulis

PRINTER: Hope Press

BUDGET: Design: $3450;

printing: $1400

PRINTING PROCESS:

2 PMS colors, offset

Image stationery that emphasizes the beauty and freshness of preliminary sketchbook drawings in pencil on tissue paper. Images were all gleaned from the illustrator's scrap files.

DESIGN FIRM:

Todd McArtor Design, Derby, Kansas

DESIGNER:

Todd McArtor

ILLUSTRATOR:

Dave LaFleur

PRINTING PROCESS:

3-color spot, 2 sides

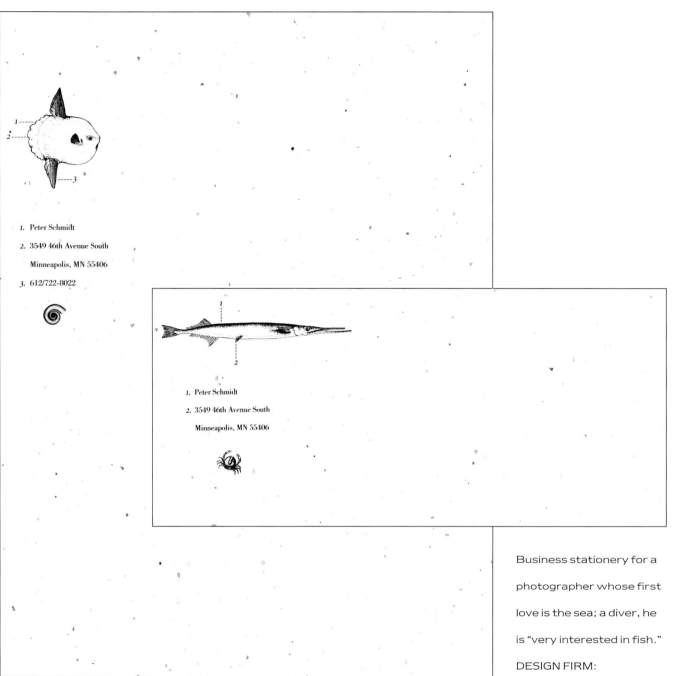

1. Peter Schmidt
2. 3549 46th Avenue South
   Minneapolis, MN 55406
3. 612/722-8022

1. Peter Schmidt
2. 3549 46th Avenue South
   Minneapolis, MN 55406

Business stationery for a photographer whose first love is the sea; a diver, he is "very interested in fish."

DESIGN FIRM:
Susan Reed Design,
Minneapolis, Minnesota
DESIGNER: Susan Reed
BUDGET: Design: pro
bono; printing: $350
PRINTING PROCESS:
1-color offset

Peter Schmidt (Commercial Photographer)

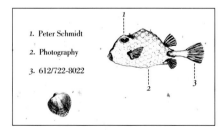

1. Peter Schmidt
2. Photography
3. 612/722-8022

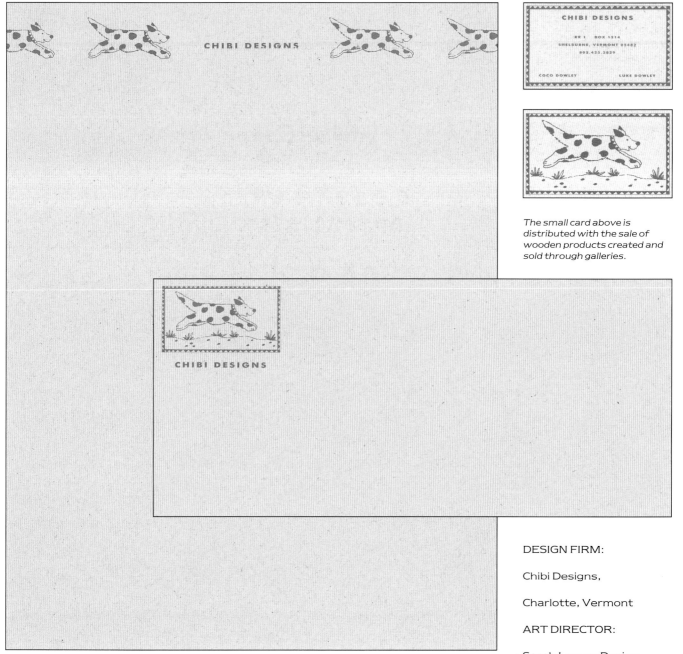

CHIBI DESIGNS

CHIBI DESIGNS

The small card above is distributed with the sale of wooden products created and sold through galleries.

CHIBI DESIGNS

Chibi Designs, Inc.

DESIGN FIRM:

Chibi Designs,

Charlotte, Vermont

ART DIRECTOR:

Sarah Larson Design,

Chicago, Illinois

DESIGNER/ILLUSTRATOR:

Coco Dowley

PRINTER: Red Star

Printing, Chicago, Illinois

BUDGET: Design: $1500;

printing: $1000

PRINTING PROCESS:

1 PMS color

Left: back of stationery.

ANDREW GOODMAN

MICHAEL LERNER

Personal correspondence script cards inspired by the company logo. The figures are from a font of type ornaments produced by America Type Foundry in the 1940s. They are from the Calendar Silhouette Series J.

DESIGN FIRM:
Zida Borcich Letterpress,
Fort Bragg, California

ART DIRECTOR/
DESIGNER: Zida Borcich

Paradesa Media (Educational and Consumer Multimedia Product Development)

ILLUSTRATORS:
Andy Goodman,
Michael Lerner

BUDGET: $700

PRINTING PROCESS:
Hand-set lead type
printed on Heidelberg
Windmill; all letterpress-
printed on recycled paper
(Speckletone Kraft)

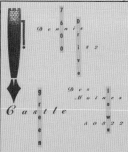

In days of old and eras long past, when kings ruled realms and spells were cast, castles were built of mortar and stone and the rulers fought for a kingdom to own. Today's castles flourish only in the minds of the dreamers and bards of our present time. But time streams merge in the mind of one wh... glow in the sun. ...the present and j... ask her to man... projects conceiv... need planning, ... Let Dawn slay ...ads, of public ...ations and promotions in scads. She'll tell your story, if that's what you want, in features, reports, documents and charts. Building a castle takes time and devotion as do projects of communication perfection. CastleGreen is Dawn's dream, a place of glory. While she builds it, let her tell your story.

A sample of Dawn Bowman's writing appears on the reverse side of her stationery.

DESIGN FIRM:

Sayles Graphic Design, Des Moines, Iowa

DESIGNER: John Sayles

PRINTING PROCESS:

1-color, offset

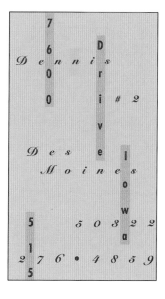

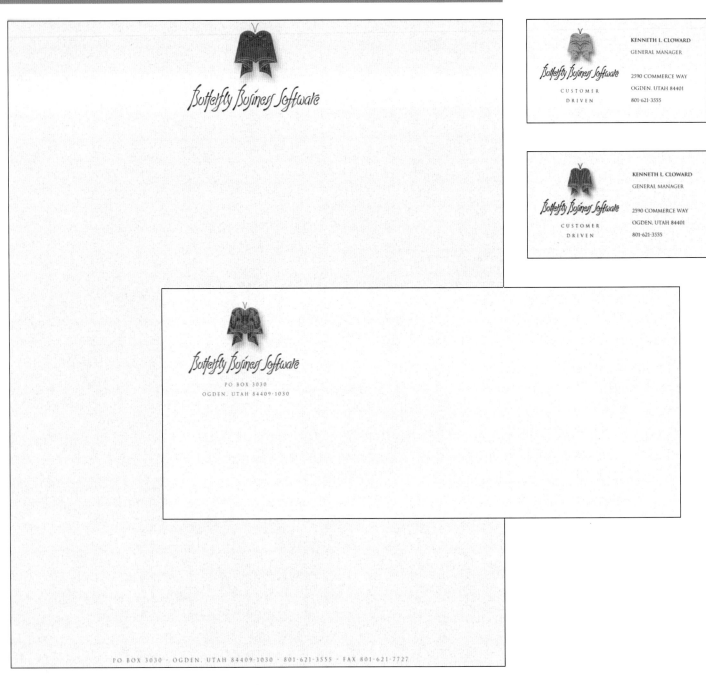

DESIGN FIRM:

Evans Group,

Salt Lake City, Utah

ART DIRECTOR/

DESIGNER/ILLUSTRATOR:

Dan Ruesch

PRINTER: Precision Litho,

Salt Lake City, Utah

BUDGET: Design: $5000;

printing: $3000

PRINTING PROCESS:

4-color

GIBSON & ROBBINS-PENNIMAN

ATTORNEYS AT LAW

J. MILES GIBSON

GUS ROBBINS-PENNIMAN

JOSEPH M. REIDY

673 SOUTH MOHAWK STREET

4TH FLOOR

COLUMBUS, OHIO 43206

614-445-5858

FAX 614-445-5850

GIBSON & ROBBINS-PENNIMAN
ATTORNEYS AT LAW
Cynthia C. Lambert
673 SOUTH MOHAWK STREET • 4TH FLOOR • COLUMBUS, OHIO 43206
614-445-5858 • FAX 614-445-5850

GIBSON & ROBBINS-PENNIMAN
ATTORNEYS AT LAW
222 HIGH STREET • SUITE 220 • HAMILTON, OHIO 45012

HAMILTON OFFICE:

222 HIGH STREET

SUITE 220

HAMILTON, OHIO 45012

513-867-8400

FAX 513-867-1176

Stationery promotes

the image of a progressive

law firm.

DESIGN FIRM:

Salvato & Coe Associates,

Columbus, Ohio

ART DIRECTOR/

DESIGNER:

Michael Dexter

BUDGET: $3500

PRINTING PROCESS:

5 flat PMS colors

Package presents a
professional image for a
public relations/
marketing consultant and
conference planner who
runs her business from
her home.
DESIGN FIRM:
Kapp & Associates, Inc.,

Cleveland, Ohio
ART DIRECTOR:
Cathryn Kapp
DESIGNER: Tim Lachina
BUDGET: Design: $6000;
printing: $3000
PRINTING PROCESS:
4 PMS colors + blind
embossing

Judith Ruggie

JUDITH RUGGIE ENTERPRISES

Judith Ruggie
President

3085 Lander Road
Cleveland, Ohio 44124
Telephone 216 360.9323
Fax 216 360.9348

JUDITH RUGGIE ENTERPRISES

3085 Lander Road
Cleveland, Ohio 44124
Telephone 216 360.9323
Fax 216 360.9348

JUDITH RUGGIE ENTERPRISES

3085 Lander Road
Cleveland, Ohio 44124

Versatile stationery developed for a new studio. Anticipating a possible move, the hand-written type allowed for any new address to be re-photocopied onto the bottom of letterhead.
ART DIRECTOR/ DESIGNER/ILLUSTRATOR: Kelley Lynch
BUDGET: Design: $385 (in-house expense); printing: $220 (paper and printing)
PRINTING PROCESS: 1-color, black, offset; hand-colored in pencil

Kelley Lynch (Artist/Graphic Designer/Illustrator)

Card in four different color combinations is used as an incentive to clients to call back with more work in order to collect all four cards.

DESIGN FIRM:

Thauer Art Direction, Milwaukee, Wisconsin

DESIGNER: Julie Thauer

PRINTER: HM Graphics

BUDGET: Bartered

PRINTING PROCESS: 4-color

Cards are handed out by existing customers and associates as referrals.

DESIGN FIRM:

Sandstrom Design, Portland, Oregon

DESIGNER:

Steve Sandstrom

COPYWRITER:

Steve Sandoz

BUDGET: No budget— design: trade-out for haircuts; printing: ran card on trim of another project's press sheet.

PRINTING PROCESS:

Offset (black + PMS red)

Judi Boldt (Hair Designer)

I know this doesn't look like a business card, I mean it's the right shape and all, but other than that it lacks most of the things that usually holler "business card" like a fancy, very expensive, lacquered, embossed, six color, die cut logo or some silly design twist on the business name. For instance, this card is for a woman who is really good at cutting hair named **Judi Boldt**, so typically this card might have pictures of bolts with different haircuts or bolts and scissors flying through space or some other stupid mnemonic device adorning it to try to get you to remember that Judi is a damn fine person to **cut your hair** and it's really

worth a trip way the hell out to **Gateway** to see her. In fact, a really creative designer might bag the business card idea altogether and simply send you a bolt in the mail with Judi's name attached. But like Judi's hair styling, we wanted this card to be memorable but not too affected so we decided to just fill it with words. That way you won't be able to use it to write down someone else's number. And maybe, just maybe, when you look in your wallet and spy this solid block of type you'll recall that visiting **Judi Boldt**, like reading, is good for your head and you'll call her right away at **252-6110** to make an appointment. At least that's our theory.

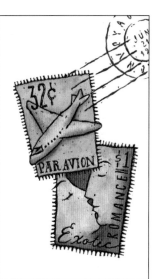

Card printed with different illustrations on the reverse side serves as a mini-portfolio.

DESIGN FIRM:

Susan Gross Illustration/Design, San Francisco, California

ART DIRECTOR/ DESIGNER/ILLUSTRATOR:

Susan Gross

BUDGET: Printing: $1000 and ganged up on a single sheet with other artists' jobs.

PRINTING PROCESS:

4-color offset

Susan Gross (Illustration/Design)

SuSan GroSS

532 Cabrillo S.f. Ca 94118
fon 415.751.5879 fax 5876

Business card in this stationery package promotes copywriter with a funny true story.

DESIGN FIRM: Mullen, Wenham, Massachusetts

ART DIRECTOR/

COPYWRITER/

ILLUSTRATOR:

Dave Swartz

BUDGET: Printing: $500

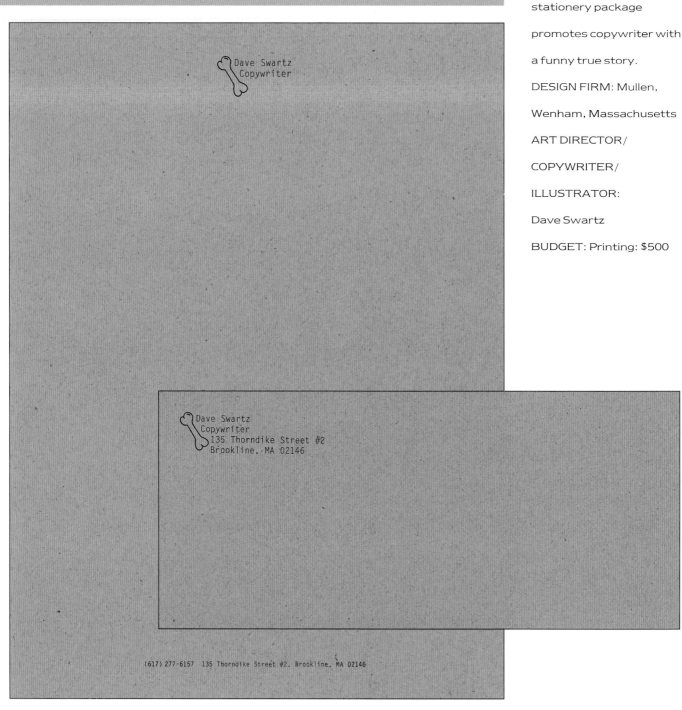

Dave Swartz
Copywriter

Dave Swartz
Copywriter
135 Thorndike Street #2
Brookline, MA 02146

(617) 277-6157 135 Thorndike Street #2, Brookline, MA 02146

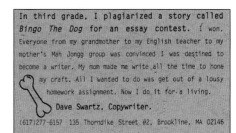

In third grade, I plagiarized a story called *Bingo The Dog* for an essay contest. I won. Everyone from my grandmother to my English teacher to my mother's Mah Jongg group was convinced I was destined to become a writer. My mom made me write all the time to hone my craft. All I wanted to do was get out of a lousy homework assignment. Now I do it for a living.

Dave Swartz, Copywriter.

(617)277-6157 135 Thorndike Street #2, Brookline, MA 02146

Patrick Jennings (Copywriter)

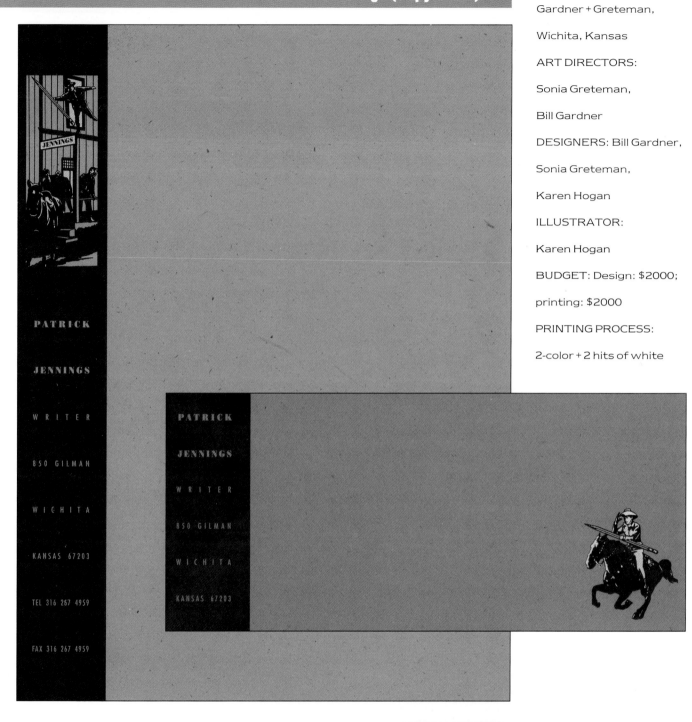

DESIGN FIRM:
Gardner + Greteman,
Wichita, Kansas
ART DIRECTORS:
Sonia Greteman,
Bill Gardner
DESIGNERS: Bill Gardner,
Sonia Greteman,
Karen Hogan
ILLUSTRATOR:
Karen Hogan
BUDGET: Design: $2000;
printing: $2000
PRINTING PROCESS:
2-color + 2 hits of white

PATRICK

JENNINGS

WRITER

850 GILMAN

WICHITA

KANSAS 67203

TEL 316 267 4959

FAX 316 267 4959

PATRICK

JENNINGS

WRITER

850 GILMAN

WICHITA

KANSAS 67203

TEL 316 267 4959

FAX 316 267 4959

23

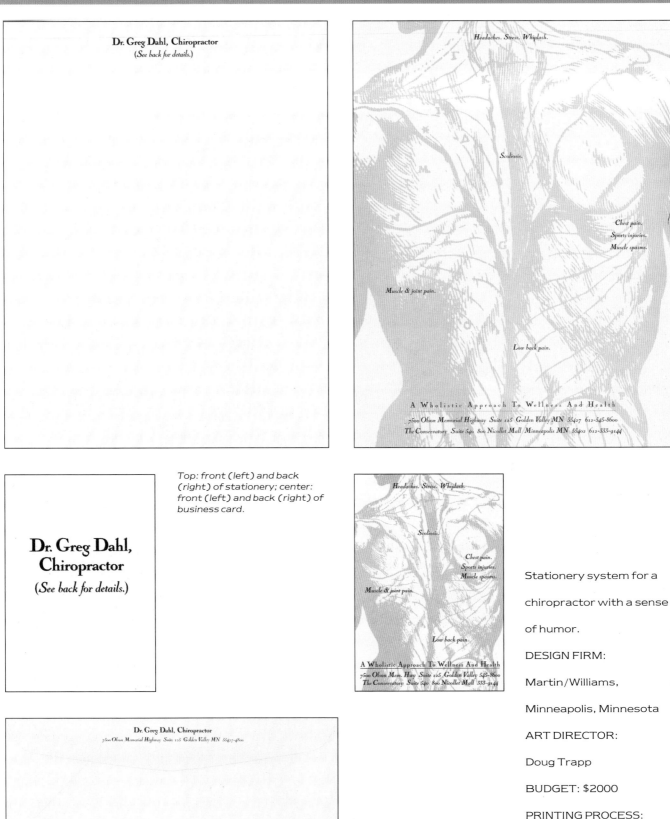

Dr. Greg Dahl, Chiropractor
(See back for details.)

Headaches. Stress. Whiplash.

Scoliosis.

Chest pain.
Sports injuries.
Muscle spasms.

Muscle & joint pain.

Low back pain.

A Wholistic Approach To Wellness And Health
7500 Olson Memorial Highway Suite 125 Golden Valley MN 55427 612-545-8600
The Conservatory Suite 540 800 Nicollet Mall Minneapolis MN 55402 612-333-9144

Top: front (left) and back (right) of stationery; center: front (left) and back (right) of business card.

Dr. Greg Dahl,
Chiropractor
(See back for details.)

Headaches. Stress. Whiplash.

Scoliosis.

Chest pain.
Sports injuries.
Muscle spasms.

Muscle & joint pain.

Low back pain.

A Wholistic Approach To Wellness And Health
7500 Olson Mem. Hwy Suite 125 Golden Valley 545-8600
The Conservatory Suite 540 800 Nicollet Mall 333-9144

Stationery system for a

chiropractor with a sense

of humor.

DESIGN FIRM:

Martin/Williams,

Minneapolis, Minnesota

ART DIRECTOR:

Doug Trapp

BUDGET: $2000

PRINTING PROCESS:

2-color

Dr. Greg Dahl, Chiropractor
7500 Olson Memorial Highway Suite 125 Golden Valley MN 55427-4800

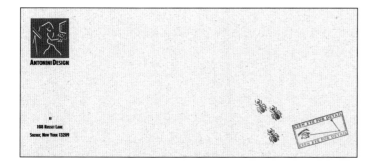

ANTONINI DESIGN

Susan Antonini
Creative Director

108 RUSSET LANE
SOLVAY, NEW YORK 13209
315 488 1849
FAX: 487 4983

Changing rubber-stamp designs give the appearance of a 4-color job.

DESIGN FIRM: Antonini Design, Solvay, New York

DESIGNERS: Susan Antonini, Carrie Childs

ILLUSTRATOR: Susan Antonini

BUDGET: Printing: $300; stamps: $12

PRINTING PROCESS: 2-color; stamps provided additional colors using Dr. Martins dyes.

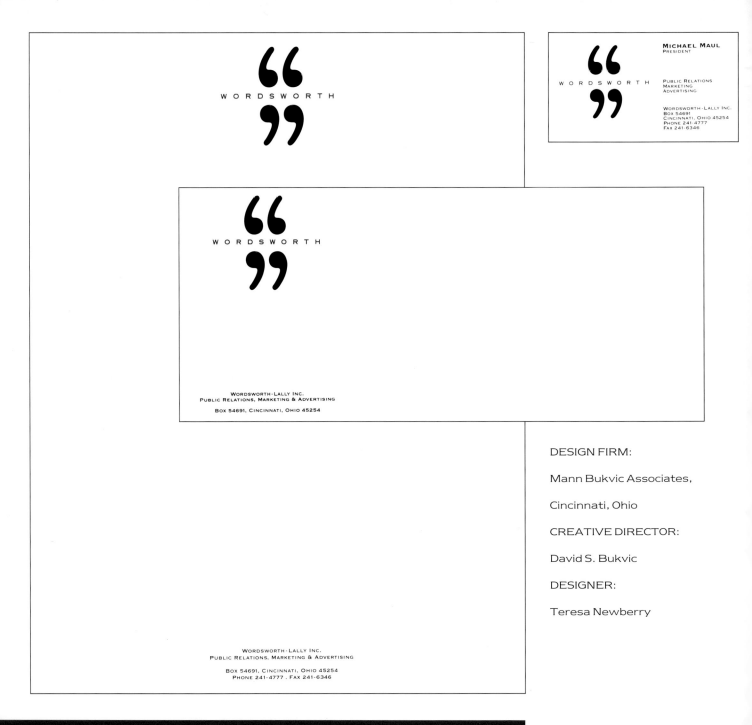

WORDSWORTH

MICHAEL MAUL
PRESIDENT

WORDSWORTH

PUBLIC RELATIONS
MARKETING
ADVERTISING

WORDSWORTH-LALLY INC.
BOX 54691
CINCINNATI, OHIO 45254
PHONE 241-4777
FAX 241-6346

WORDSWORTH

WORDSWORTH-LALLY INC.
PUBLIC RELATIONS, MARKETING & ADVERTISING

BOX 54691, CINCINNATI, OHIO 45254

DESIGN FIRM:

Mann Bukvic Associates,

Cincinnati, Ohio

CREATIVE DIRECTOR:

David S. Bukvic

DESIGNER:

Teresa Newberry

WORDSWORTH-LALLY INC.
PUBLIC RELATIONS, MARKETING & ADVERTISING

BOX 54691, CINCINNATI, OHIO 45254
PHONE 241-4777 . FAX 241-6346

Wordsworth-Lally Inc. (Public Relations)

WORDSWORTH

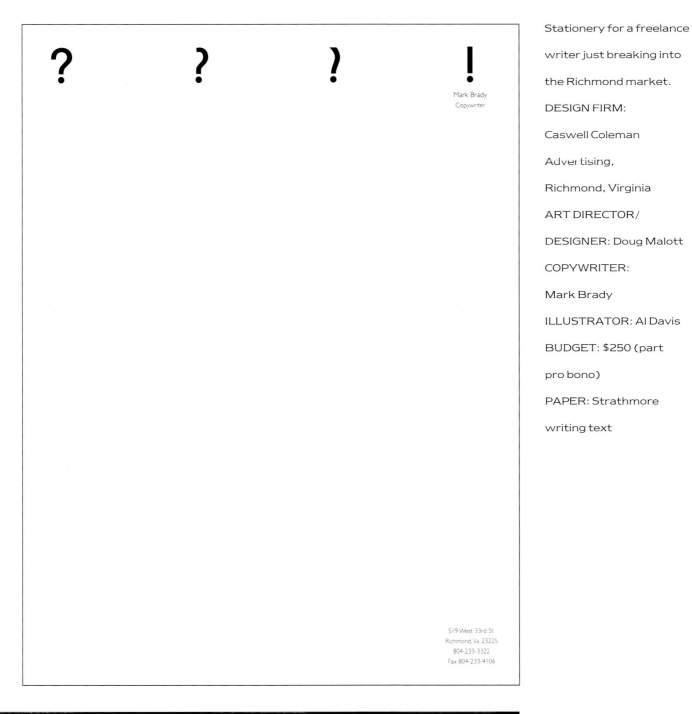

? ? ? !

Mark Brady
Copywriter

519 West 33rd St.
Richmond, Va 23225
804-233-3322
Fax 804-233-4106

Stationery for a freelance writer just breaking into the Richmond market.
DESIGN FIRM:
Caswell Coleman Advertising, Richmond, Virginia
ART DIRECTOR/ DESIGNER: Doug Malott
COPYWRITER: Mark Brady
ILLUSTRATOR: Al Davis
BUDGET: $250 (part pro bono)
PAPER: Strathmore writing text

Mark Brady (Copywriter)

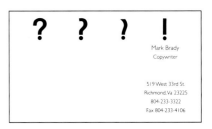

? ? ? !

Mark Brady
Copywriter

519 West 33rd St.
Richmond, Va 23225
804-233-3322
Fax 804-233-4106

27

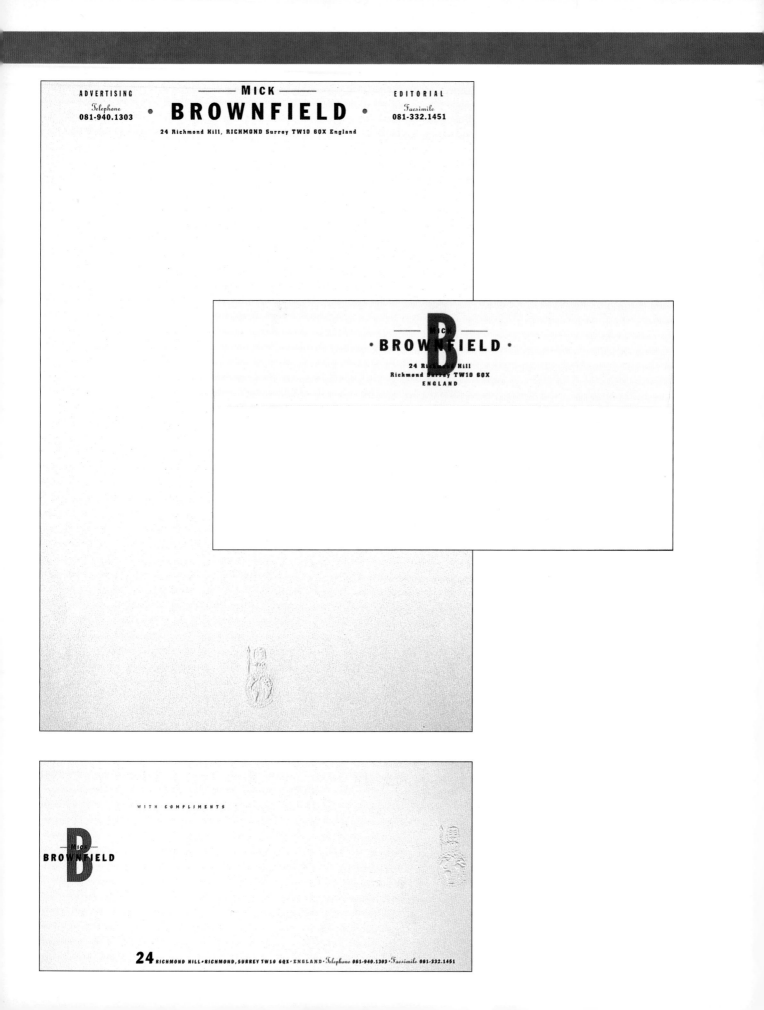

TELEPHONE #
081-940.1303

FACSIMILE #
081-332.1451

DATE: ....

TO: ....

ATTN: ....

NO. OF PAGES (INCLUDING THIS ONE) ....

MICK BROWNFIELD 24 RICHMOND HILL, RICHMOND, SURREY TW10 6QX · ENGLAND ·

This stationery package reflects Mick Brownfield's status as a top European advertising and editorial illustrator.

DESIGN FIRM: Ph.D, Santa Monica, California

ART DIRECTOR/ DESIGNER: Clive Piercy

CO-ART DIRECTOR: Michael Hodgson

BUDGET: Design: $2500; printing: $2500

PRINTING PROCESS: 3-color, offset + blind embossing

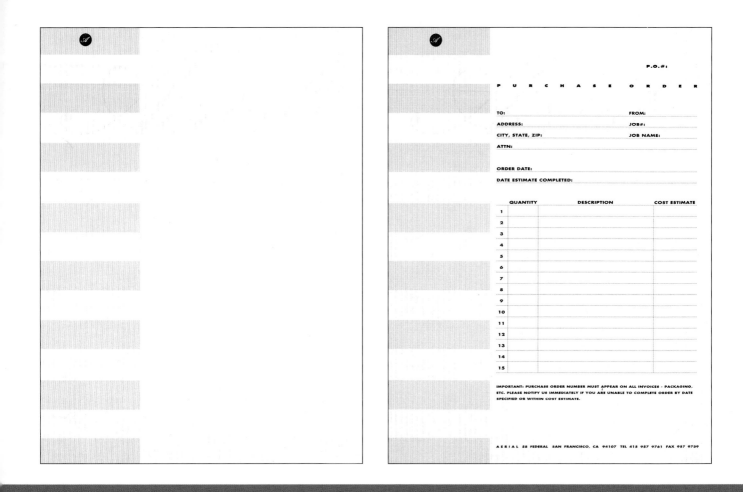

P.O.#:

P U R C H A S E   O R D E R

TO: FROM:

ADDRESS: JOB#:

CITY, STATE, ZIP: JOB NAME:

ATTN:

ORDER DATE:

DATE ESTIMATE COMPLETED:

	QUANTITY	DESCRIPTION	COST ESTIMATE
1			
2			
3			
4			
5			
6			
7			
8			
9			
10			
11			
12			
13			
14			
15			

IMPORTANT: PURCHASE ORDER NUMBER MUST APPEAR ON ALL INVOICES - PACKAGING,
ETC. PLEASE NOTIFY US IMMEDIATELY IF YOU ARE UNABLE TO COMPLETE ORDER BY DATE
SPECIFIED OR WITHIN COST ESTIMATS.

AERIAL 58 FEDERAL SAN FRANCISCO, CA 94107 TEL 415 957 9761 FAX 957 9739

AERIAL FIFTY-EIGHT FEDERAL
SAN FRANCISCO CA 94107-1432

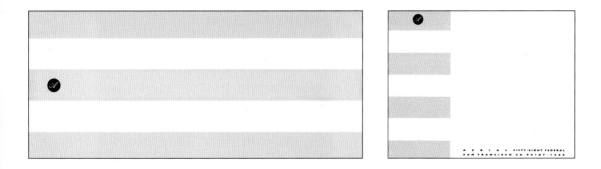

A E R I A L (Identity Consultants)

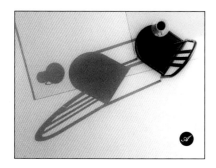

This package provides an overview or *A E R I A L* perspective on identity issues for clients. The business card series, which grows yearly, shows various aerial views of imagery, promoting the firm's viewpoint and special perspective.
DESIGN FIRM: A E R I A L, San Francisco, California

ART DIRECTOR/ DESIGNER: Tracy Moon
PHOTOGRAPHER: R. J. Muna
SEPARATIONS: ReproMedia, Inc.
PRINTING PROCESS: Business cards: 4-color + dull varnish over 1 PMS; stationery: 2 PMS over 1 PMS (letterhead)

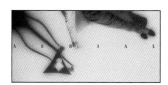

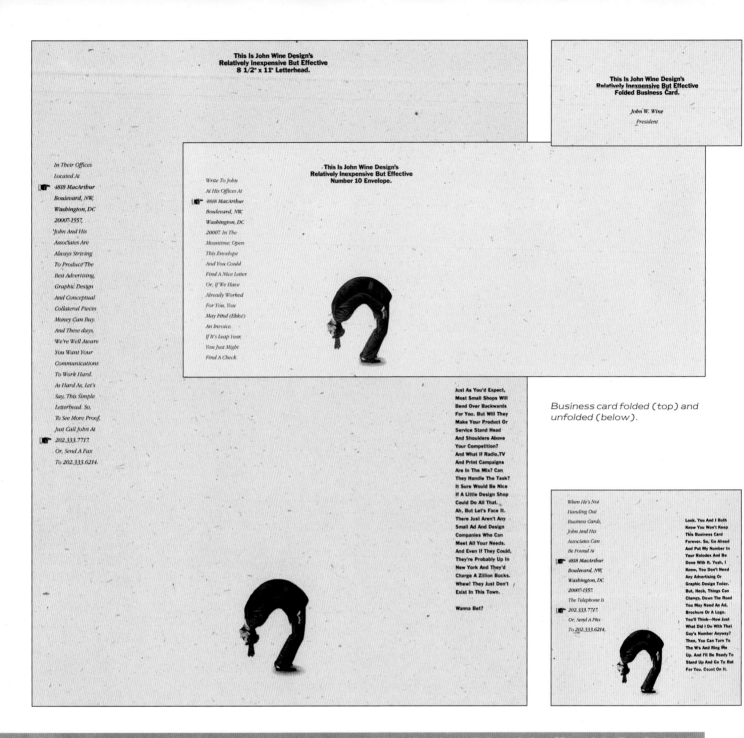

Business card folded (top) and unfolded (below).

John Wine Design (Advertising/Graphic Design)

Portrays an image of a designer who will bend over backwards to service the client, and at the same time produce effective, creative, and result-oriented advertising and design.

DESIGN FIRM: John Wine Design, Washington, DC

ART DIRECTOR/ DESIGNER: John Wine

PHOTOGRAPHER: Carl Fischer

PRINTING PROCESS: Envelopes: 1-color, offset; cards/letters: 600 dpi laser printer

32

Conveys the distinguished
quality of this English
copywriter's work.
DESIGN FIRM:
Mires Design,
San Diego, California
ART DIRECTOR/
DESIGNER: Scott Mires

Brian Meredith (Copywriter)

ILLUSTRATOR:
Seymour Chwast
PRINTING PROCESS:
4-color

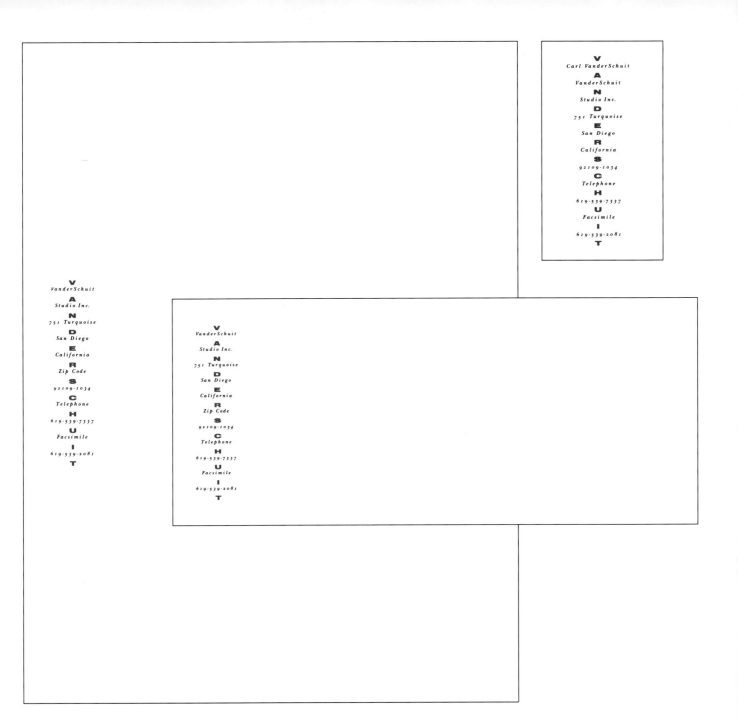

Carl VanderSchuit (Photographer)

DESIGN FIRM:

Mires Design,

San Diego, California

ART DIRECTOR/

DESIGNER: José Serrano

PRINTING PROCESS:

2-color

Graphica   Design and   4501 Lyons Rd.
            Communications   Miamisburg, OH 45342
            Group   513-866-4013

Graphica   Design and
            Communications
            Group

2501 Lyons Rd
Miamisburg, OH 45342
513-866-4013
513-866-5581 Fax

Geoff Reichel
Designer

Graphica   Design and   4501 Lyons Rd.
            Communications   Miamisburg, OH 45342
            Group

Graphica, Inc. (Graphic Design)

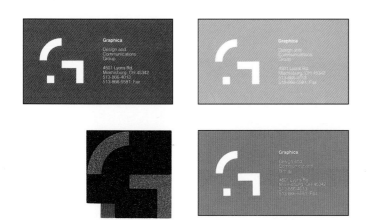

DESIGN FIRM:

Graphica, Inc.,

Miamisburg, Ohio

ART DIRECTOR:

Nick Stamas

DESIGNER: Geoff Reichel

PRINTING PROCESS:

3 flat colors, offset

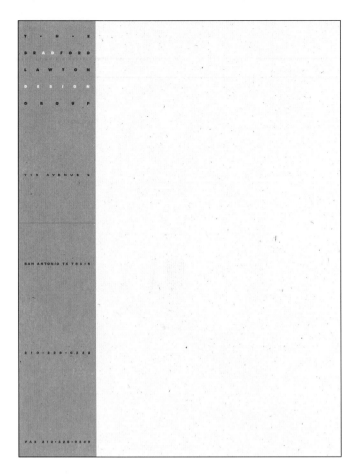

The Bradford Lawton Design Group

Above: front and back of stationery.

DESIGN FIRM:

Bradford Lawton Design

Group, San Antonio, Texas

ART DIRECTORS:

Brad Lawton,

Jennifer Griffith-Garcia

DESIGNERS/

ILLUSTRATORS:

Brad Lawton, Jody Laney

PRINTING PROCESS:

3-color

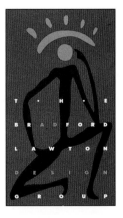

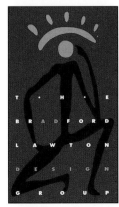

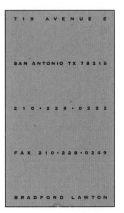

DESIGN FIRM:

Wilcox Design,

Atlanta, Georgia

DESIGNER/ILLUSTRATOR:

Mark Wilcox

BUDGET: $2800

PRINTING PROCESS:

2 PMS colors, lithography

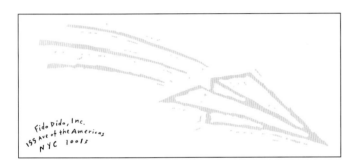

Fido Dido, Inc.
155 Ave of the Americas
NYC 10013
fone 212 929 5099
fax 212 366 6264

please
work over the
dough

Date:

Invoice No:

Client:

Contact:

Client Job No:

Fido Job No:

Date sent:

Job Description:

Total:

Please remit within 30 days of invoice date.

Thanks.

Fido Dido, Inc.
155 Ave of the Americas
NYC 10013

Fido Dido, Inc. (Licensed Comic Property)

Fido Dido, Inc.
155 Ave of the Americas
NYC 10013
fone 212 929 5099

Stationery is meant to be
mixed and matched.
DESIGN FIRM:
Fido Dido, Inc.,
New York, New York
ART DIRECTOR/
DESIGNER/ILLUSTRATOR:
Susan Rose
PRINTING PROCESS:
Offset; each piece was
printed using black and a
second color (5 in all).

39

Above: front and back of business card.

Melissa Salengo
Designer O'Stuff

BEN & JERRY'S®
VERMONT'S FINEST • ICE CREAM & FROZEN YOGURT™

P.O. Box 240
Waterbury, VT 05676
Tel. 802/244-6957
Fax. 802/244-5944

Business card design commemorates the company's outreach program to Russia.

DESIGN FIRM:

Ben & Jerry's

Creative Department,

Waterbury, Vermont

ART DIRECTOR:

Lyn Severance

DESIGNER: Sarah Forbes

ILLUSTRATOR:

Melissa Salengo

PRINTING PROCESS:

4-color

DESIGN FIRM:

Kenney & Westmark,

Pensacola, Florida

ART DIRECTOR/

DESIGNER: John Westmark

BUDGET: Design: tradeout

for food; printing: $200

(for 500)

PRINTING PROCESS:

3-color (PMS); used stock

printer had on floor from

previous job.

DESIGN FIRM:

Gibbs Baronet,

Dallas, Texas

ART DIRECTORS:

Willie Baronet, Steve Gibbs

DESIGNER: Willie Baronet

BUDGET: $500

PRINTING PROCESS:

2-color (PMS)

Max Wright (Copywriter)

Translator/interpreter for Spanish-, Italian-, French- and German-speaking clients in the Maryland court system.

DESIGN FIRM: Studio A, Alexandria, Virginia

ART DIRECTOR/ DESIGNER: Antonio Alcalá

BUDGET: $0; card was printed along with reprints of Studio A's business cards.

PRINTING PROCESS: 2-color, offset

JORGE H. ALCALÁ

INTERPRETER · TRANSLATOR

514 VALLEYWOOD ROAD · MILLERSVILLE MD 21108   410·987·5228

Jorge H. Alcalá

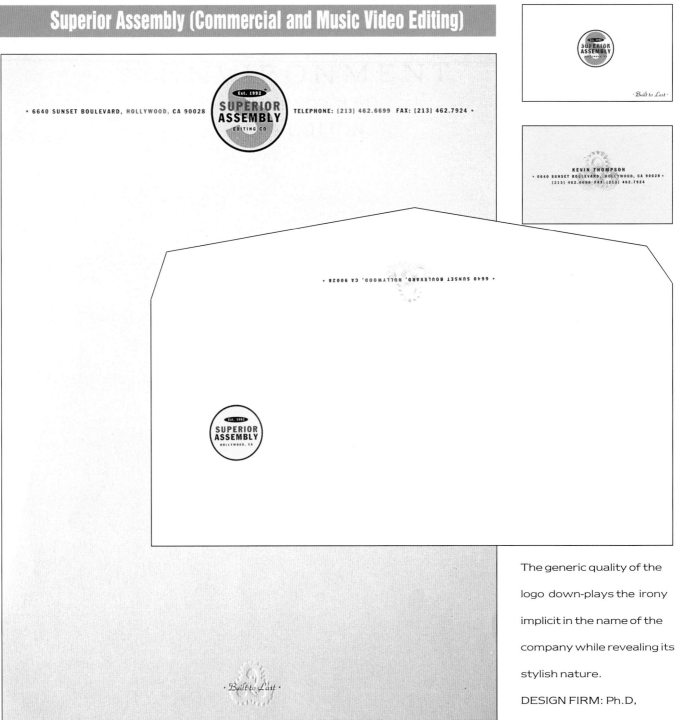

The generic quality of the logo down-plays the irony implicit in the name of the company while revealing its stylish nature.

DESIGN FIRM: Ph.D, Santa Monica, California

ART DIRECTORS: Clive Piercy, Michael Hodgson

ILLUSTRATOR: George Hardie

PRINTING PROCESS: 4-color, offset + blind embossing

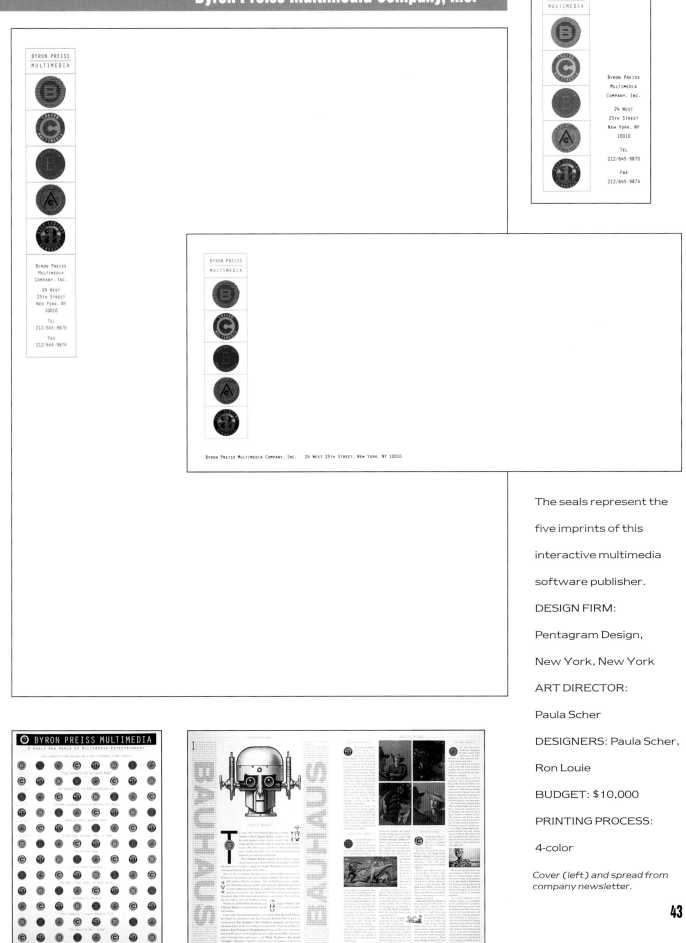

The seals represent the
five imprints of this
interactive multimedia
software publisher.

DESIGN FIRM:

Pentagram Design,

New York, New York

ART DIRECTOR:

Paula Scher

DESIGNERS: Paula Scher,

Ron Louie

BUDGET: $10,000

PRINTING PROCESS:

4-color

*Cover (left) and spread from
company newsletter.*

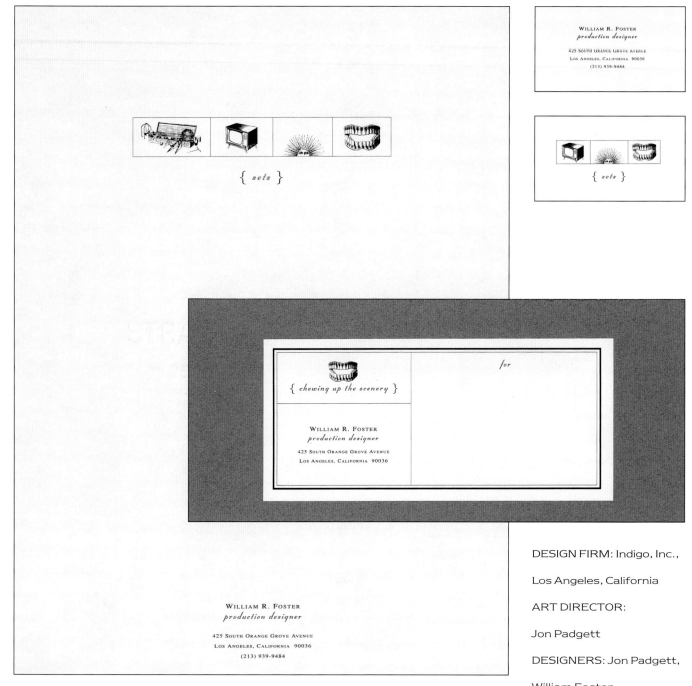

William R. Foster (Television/Film Scenic Designer)

DESIGN FIRM: Indigo, Inc.,

Los Angeles, California

ART DIRECTOR:

Jon Padgett

DESIGNERS: Jon Padgett,

William Foster

BUDGET: Design: pro bono;

printing: $500

PRINTING PROCESS:

1-color, offset

44

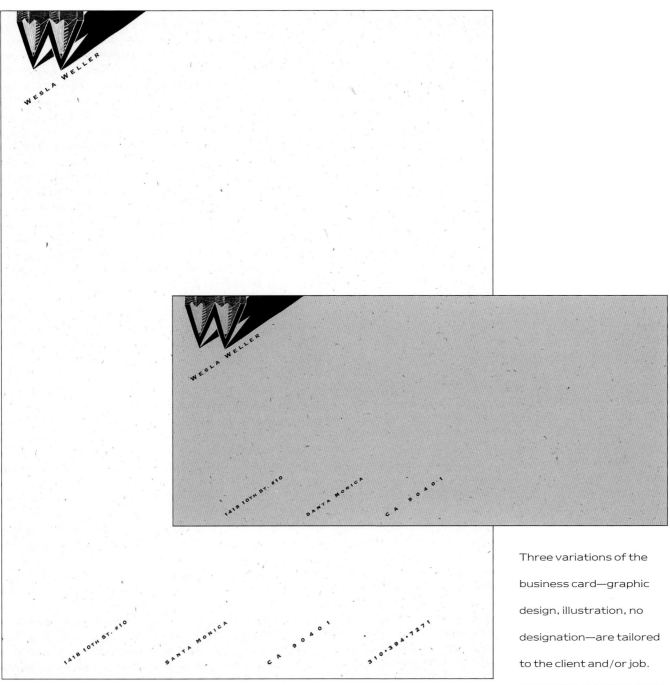

Wesla Weller (Graphic Designer/Illustrator)

Three variations of the business card—graphic design, illustration, no designation—are tailored to the client and/or job. DESIGNER/ILLUSTRATOR: Wesla Weller, Santa Monica, California PRINTING PROCESS: Black ink, offset + hand-coloring (Prismacolor pencil)

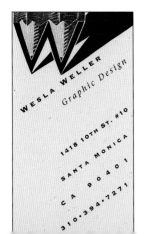

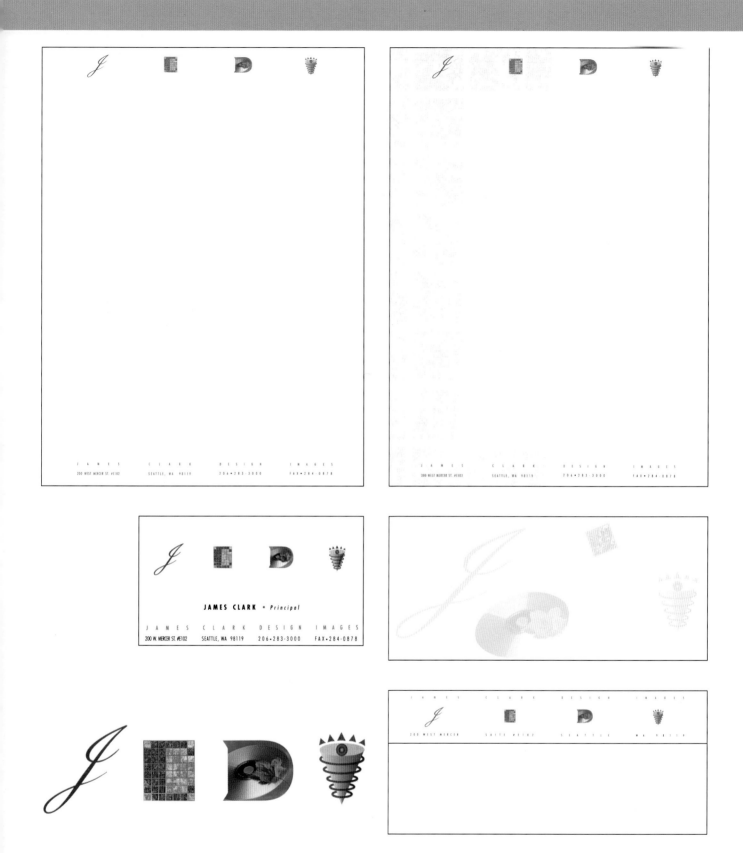

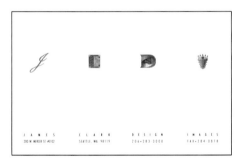

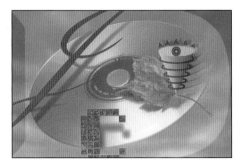

Stationery package uses four different icons to represent individual aspects of this firm—*J* for classic type, *C* for textural, *D* for digital future and *I* for fun.

DESIGN FIRM:

James Clark

Design Images,

Seattle, Washington

DESIGNER: James Clark

ILLUSTRATOR:

Dyanna Kosak

PRINTING PROCESS:

4-color + 1 PMS, offset

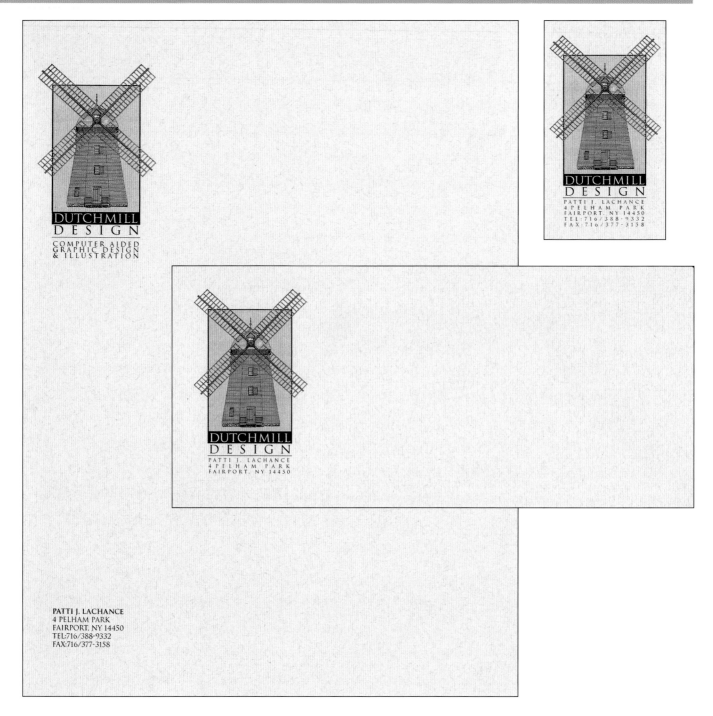

Stationery expresses the design flavor and illustrative approach of a small freelance studio, as well as its technical capabilities.

DESIGN FIRM:

Dutchmill Design, Fairport, New York

ART DIRECTOR/ DESIGNER:

Patti Lachance

BUDGET: Design: $700; printing: $1500 (for 500 of each)

PRINTING PROCESS:

Xerox 5775 color laser output, 1600 x 400 dpi

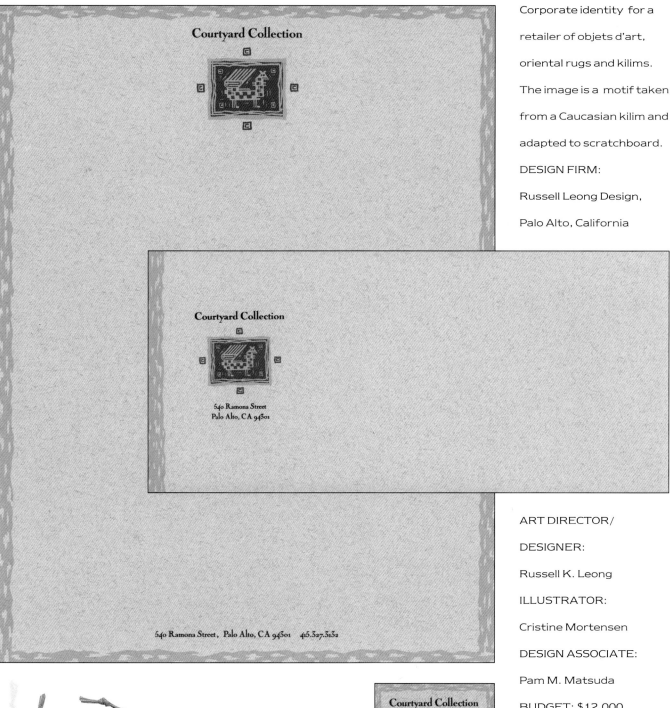

Corporate identity for a retailer of objets d'art, oriental rugs and kilims. The image is a motif taken from a Caucasian kilim and adapted to scratchboard.

DESIGN FIRM:

Russell Leong Design,

Palo Alto, California

ART DIRECTOR/

DESIGNER:

Russell K. Leong

ILLUSTRATOR:

Cristine Mortensen

DESIGN ASSOCIATE:

Pam M. Matsuda

BUDGET: $12,000

PRINTING PROCESS:

3-color, offset

Hangtags.

MDB Limited   Project   4121 Whiting Court   Phn 703.680.3703
                     Management   Woodbridge, VA   Fax 703.730.0485
                                      22193

MDB Limited   Project   4121 Whiting Court
               Management   Woodbridge, VA
                                22193

The sequence of images in
the logo communicates the
idea of construction and a
sense of action.

DESIGN FIRM:

Sparkman+Associates,

Washington, DC

ART DIRECTOR/

DESIGNER: Don Sparkman

BUDGET: Design: $2500;

printing: $1200

PRINTING PROCESS:

Offset

MDB Limited (Building Contractor)

MDB Limited   4121 Whiting Court
                         Woodbridge, VA
                         22193

Michael D. Bopp   Phn 703.680.3703
President   Fax 703.730.0485

50

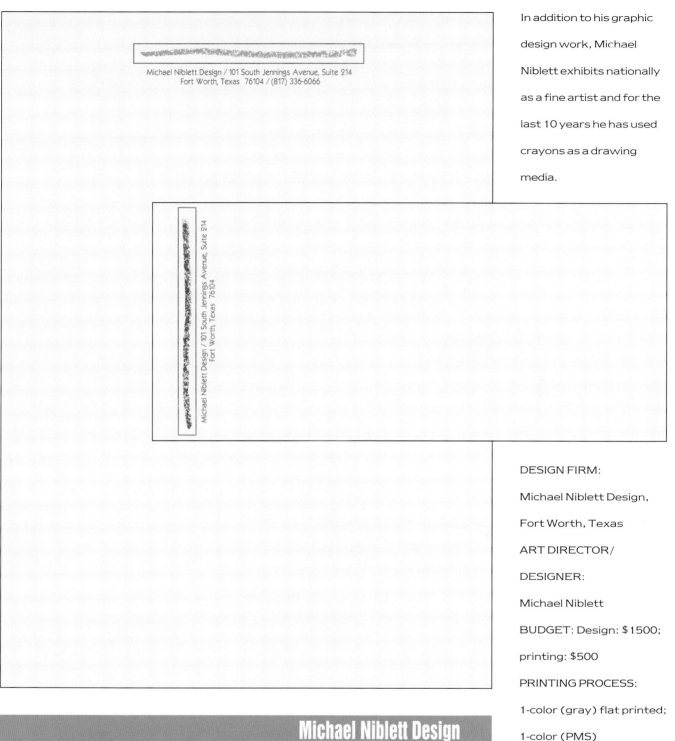

In addition to his graphic design work, Michael Niblett exhibits nationally as a fine artist and for the last 10 years he has used crayons as a drawing media.

Michael Niblett Design / 101 South Jennings Avenue, Suite 214
Fort Worth, Texas 76104 / (817) 336-6066

Michael Niblett Design / 101 South Jennings Avenue, Suite 214
Fort Worth, Texas 76104

Michael Niblett Design

DESIGN FIRM:

Michael Niblett Design,

Fort Worth, Texas

ART DIRECTOR/

DESIGNER:

Michael Niblett

BUDGET: Design: $1500;

printing: $500

PRINTING PROCESS:

1-color (gray) flat printed;

1-color (PMS)

thermographed

Michael Niblett Design / 101 South Jennings Avenue, Suite 214
Fort Worth, Texas 76104 / (817) 336-6066

DIRECTORS
MARC HALPERIN
MICHAEL PIACENTINI
JAMES REITER

MARC HALPERIN
Culinary Director

1621 MONTGOMERY STREET
SAN FRANCISCO, CALIFORNIA 94111
TEL: 415.693.8908 • FAX: 415.693.8919

1621 MONTGOMERY
SAN FRANCISCO
CALIFORNIA 94111

1621 MONTGOMERY STREET • SAN FRANCISCO, CALIFORNIA • 94111
TEL: 415.693.8900 • FAX: 415.693.8919

DESIGN FIRMS:
Rick Sams, Shelby
Designs & Illustrates,
Oakland, California
DESIGNERS: Rick Sams,
Shelby Putnam Tupper
ILLUSTRATOR: Rick Sams
PRODUCTION: E. Cotler,
Shelby Putnam Tupper
PRINTING PROCESS:
2-color, offset

Package uses the idea of the missing piece needed to solve a puzzle to promote the writer's entry into the mystery fiction market. The loose puzzle pieces (die-cut from the business cards and stationery) are often inserted into outgoing letters.

DESIGN FIRM:

Linnea Gruber Design, Imperial Beach, California

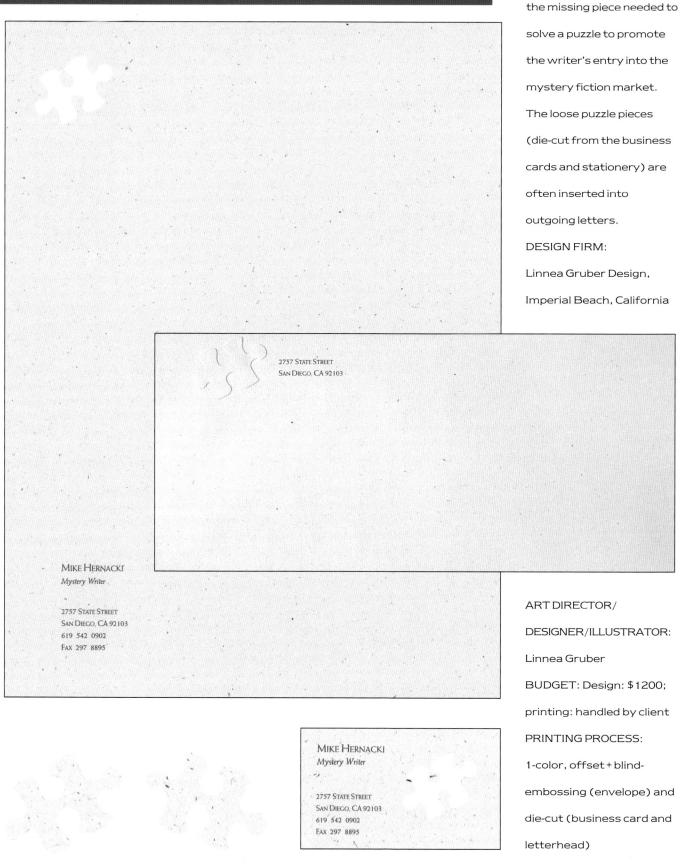

2757 State Street
San Diego, CA 92103

Mike Hernacki
Mystery Writer

2757 State Street
San Diego, CA 92103
619 542 0902
Fax 297 8895

Mike Hernacki
Mystery Writer

2757 State Street
San Diego, CA 92103
619 542 0902
Fax 297 8895

ART DIRECTOR/

DESIGNER/ILLUSTRATOR:

Linnea Gruber

BUDGET: Design: $1200;

printing: handled by client

PRINTING PROCESS:

1-color, offset + blind-embossing (envelope) and die-cut (business card and letterhead)

A & M Records
Akadama
American Cinematheque
Axlam
Bacharach & Associates
Baskin-Robbins
Blue Note Records
BodyBoarding Magazine
Breaker Jeans
Brittania Jeans
Bubble Yum
Bud Light
C&H Sugar
Camels
CBS Fox Video
CBS/Columbia Records
Chastain Shadow
Chevrolet
Chrysler Corp.
Church's Chicken
City Magazine
Coco's Restaurants
Columbia Pictures
Criswell Development Co.
D.E.G.
Disneyland
Dorman Winthrop
Embassy Pictures
Esquire
Fats Domino
Filmex
Frances Coppola
George Harrison
Giorgio
Gordon & Smith
Gotcha
Harper's Bazaar
Harry's Bar & American Grill
The Hollywood Reporter
Hot Wheels
Jack in the Box (WRG)
James Taylor
Jerry Magnin
Kaleidoscope Film
Keystone Resort
Kirin Beer
Levi Strauss (FCB Honig)
Life
Lincoln Mercury
London Sunday Times
Lorimar
Los Angeles Herald Examiner
Los Angeles Times
LucasFilm
M.C.D.
Made In the Shade Jeans
Howie Mandel
Mattel
Max Software
Medallion Books
MGM
Michael Jackson
Nalley Foods
National Endowment for the Arts
Nervous
NBC
New Horizon Pictures
New World Pictures
Newport Publications
Newsweek
O'Neill Wetsuits
O'Neal MX
Ocean Pacific Sunwear, Ltd.
Orion Pictures
Paramount Pictures
Penthouse
Petersen Publishing
Playboy
Polygram
Ponderosa Homes
Ralston-Purina
Randy Newman
RCA
Revell Toys
Rickie Lee Jones
Rolling Stone
The San Francisco Examiner
Schick
Scotti Bros. Records
Sebastian International
Software Ventures
Sony
Standard Shoes
StraightArrow Books
Surfer Magazine
Surfing Magazine
Taco Bell
TDK
Tina Turner
Tri-Star Pictures
Twentieth Century Fox
U.S. Suzuki
United Artists
Universal Studios
Vogue
Warner Bros. Pictures
Warner Bros. Records
Warner Home Video
White Water Falls
XEGM AM 95

Stationery showcases the

firm's design capabilities.

DESIGN FIRM:

Mike Salisbury

Communications, Inc.,

Torrance, California

ART DIRECTOR:

Mike Salisbury

DESIGNER/ILLUSTRATOR:

Regina Grosveld

PRINTING PROCESS:

2-color, offset

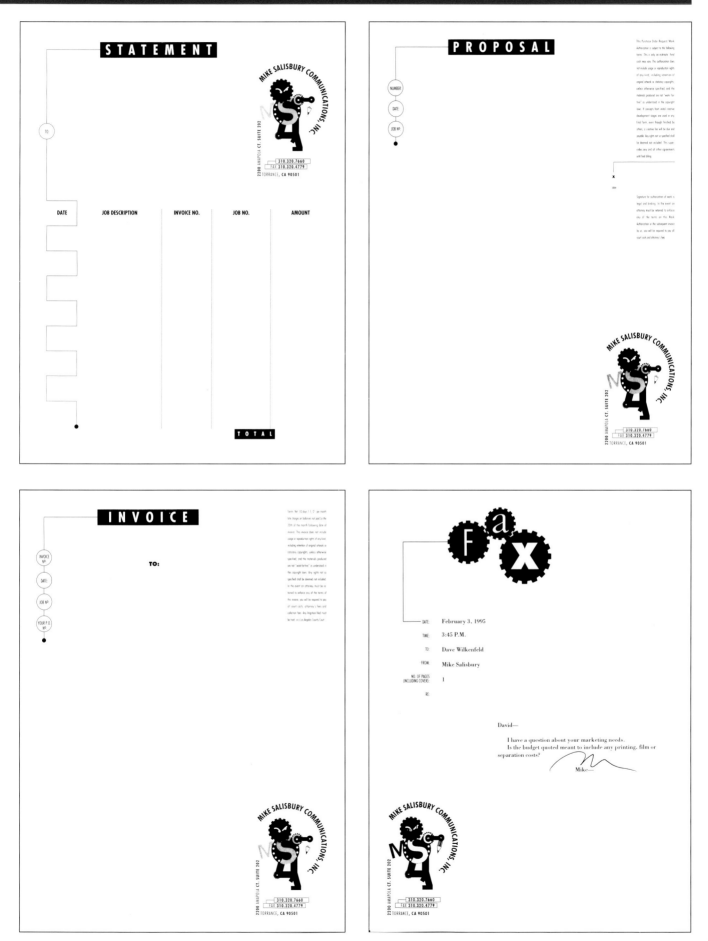

STATEMENT

MIKE SALISBURY COMMUNICATIONS, INC.

310.320.7660
FAX 310.320.4779
2200 AMAPOLA CT. SUITE 202
TORRANCE, CA 90501

TO

DATE	JOB DESCRIPTION	INVOICE NO.	JOB NO.	AMOUNT

TOTAL

PROPOSAL

NUMBER
DATE
JOB Nº

X

MIKE SALISBURY COMMUNICATIONS, INC.

310.320.7660
FAX 310.320.4779
2200 AMAPOLA CT. SUITE 202
TORRANCE, CA 90501

INVOICE

INVOICE Nº
DATE
JOB Nº
YOUR P.O. Nº

TO:

MIKE SALISBURY COMMUNICATIONS, INC.

310.320.7660
FAX 310.320.4779
2200 AMAPOLA CT. SUITE 202
TORRANCE, CA 90501

FAX

DATE: February 3, 1995
TIME: 3:45 P.M.
TO: Dave Wilkenfeld
FROM: Mike Salisbury
NO. OF PAGES
(INCLUDING COVER):   1
RE:

David—

I have a question about your marketing needs.
Is the budget quoted meant to include any printing, film or
separation costs?

Mike—

MIKE SALISBURY COMMUNICATIONS, INC.

310.320.7660
FAX 310.320.4779
2200 AMAPOLA CT. SUITE 202
TORRANCE, CA 90501

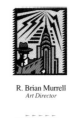

The**AD**Company

R. Brian Murrell
Art Director

1803 Hampton Street
P.O. Box 625
Columbia, SC 29202
803 • 765 • 1133
fax 803 • 252 • 6410

The**AD**Company

The**AD**Company

1803 Hampton Street
P.O. Box 625
Columbia, SC 29202
803 • 765 • 1133
fax 803 • 252 • 6410

Fold-out Christmas card.

It's Beginning   To Look A Lot   Like Christmas At   The**AD**Company

A series of four icons is used to promote and identify the firm.

DESIGN FIRM:

The AD Company, Columbia, South Carolina

ART DIRECTOR:

Brian Murrell

DESIGNER/ILLUSTRATOR:

Craig Houston

PRINTING PROCESS:

4 Pantone colors

B R O O M   &   B R O O M ,   I N C .   3 6 0   P O S T   S T R E E T

S U I T E   N O .   1 1 0 0   S A N   F R A N C I S C O

C A L I F O R N I A   9   4   1   0   8

4 1 5   3 9 7   4 3 0 0   F A X   4 1 5   3 9 7   0 6 7 0

Stationery reflects the firm's relocation to Union Square with an illustration of the locale and its prominent landmark—a statue to the veterans of the Spanish/American War. DESIGN FIRM: Broom & Broom, San Francisco, California

ART DIRECTOR: David Broom
DESIGNERS: David Broom, Deborah Hagemann
ILLUSTRATOR: Ward Schumaker
BUDGET: Design: $8500; printing: $17,000
PRINTING PROCESS: 3 PMS + black, offset (letterhead, labels, envelopes, business cards); 3 PMS + black, letterpress (moving card, envelope)

BROOM & BROOM 360 POST STREET

SUITE NO. 1100   SAN FRANCISCO

CALIFORNIA   94108

TELEPHONE 415 397 4300 FAX 415 397 0670

ALLISON CEASE

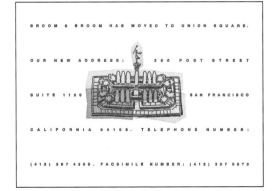

BROOM & BROOM HAS MOVED TO UNION SQUARE.

OUR NEW ADDRESS: 360 POST STREET

SUITE 1100   SAN FRANCISCO

CALIFORNIA 94108. TELEPHONE NUMBER:

(415) 397 4300. FACSIMILE NUMBER: (415) 397 0670

DEVELOPING THE TOTAL CHILD

DESIGN FIRM:

Trousdell Design, Inc.,

Atlanta, Georgia

ART DIRECTOR:

Don Trousdell

PRINTING PROCESS:

PMS colors + gold stamping

6035 Sandy Springs Circle, Atlanta, GA 30328, 404 250-1771

Kid's Business (Child Development Center)

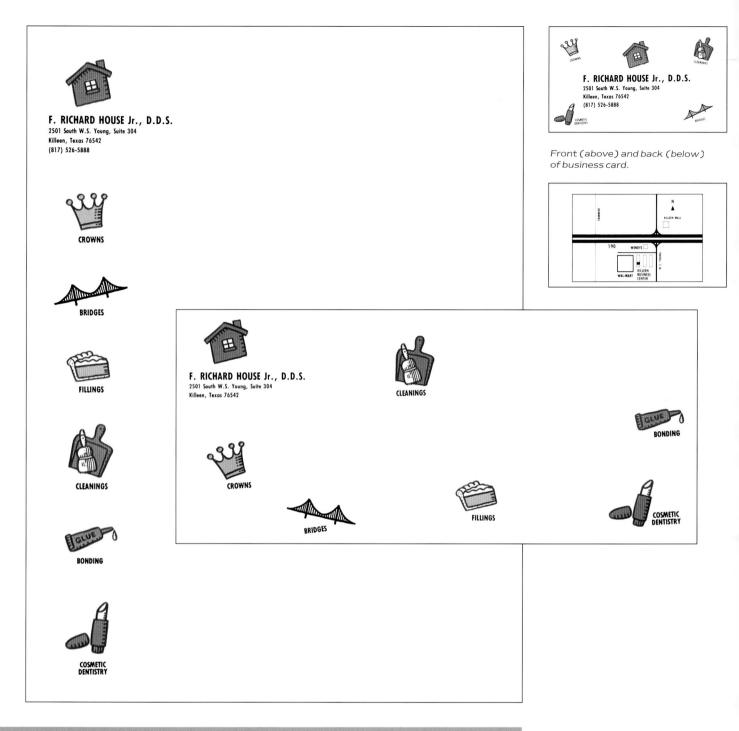

Front (above) and back (below)
of business card.

F. Richard House Jr., D.D.S.

Whimsical symbols promote Dr. House as friendly and non-threatening, soothing the anxieties people have about visiting a dentist's office.

DESIGN FIRM:
Artworks Advertising,
Killeen, Texas
ART DIRECTOR/
DESIGNER/ILLUSTRATOR:
Keith Dotson

BUDGET: $1537
(includes design,
production and printing)
PRINTING PROCESS:
Black and Pantone
vibrant colors, offset

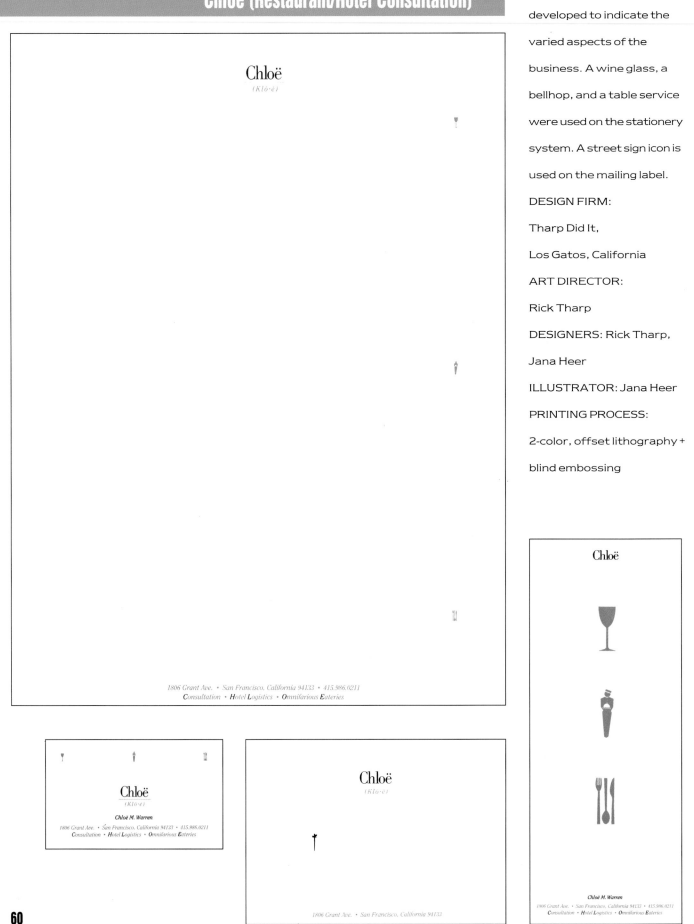

Chloë

(Klō·ē)

1806 Grant Ave. • San Francisco, California 94133 • 415.986.0211
Consultation • Hotel Logistics • Omnifarious Eateries

Chloë
(Klō·ē)

Chloë M. Warren
1806 Grant Ave. • San Francisco, California 94133 • 415.986.0211
Consultation • Hotel Logistics • Omnifarious Eateries

Chloë
(Klō·ē)

1806 Grant Ave. • San Francisco, California 94133

Chloë

Chloë M. Warren
1806 Grant Ave. • San Francisco, California 94133 • 415.986.0211
Consultation • Hotel Logistics • Omnifarious Eateries

A series of icons were developed to indicate the varied aspects of the business. A wine glass, a bellhop, and a table service were used on the stationery system. A street sign icon is used on the mailing label.

DESIGN FIRM:

Tharp Did It,

Los Gatos, California

ART DIRECTOR:

Rick Tharp

DESIGNERS: Rick Tharp,

Jana Heer

ILLUSTRATOR: Jana Heer

PRINTING PROCESS:

2-color, offset lithography +

blind embossing

Self-promotional stationery based on the actual meaning of the designer's last name—Czech for "one who is hunted." The target perforation is done individually by hand.

ART DIRECTOR/ DESIGNER: Tom Stvan, New York, New York

BUDGET: Printing: $400

PRINTING PROCESS: 2-color

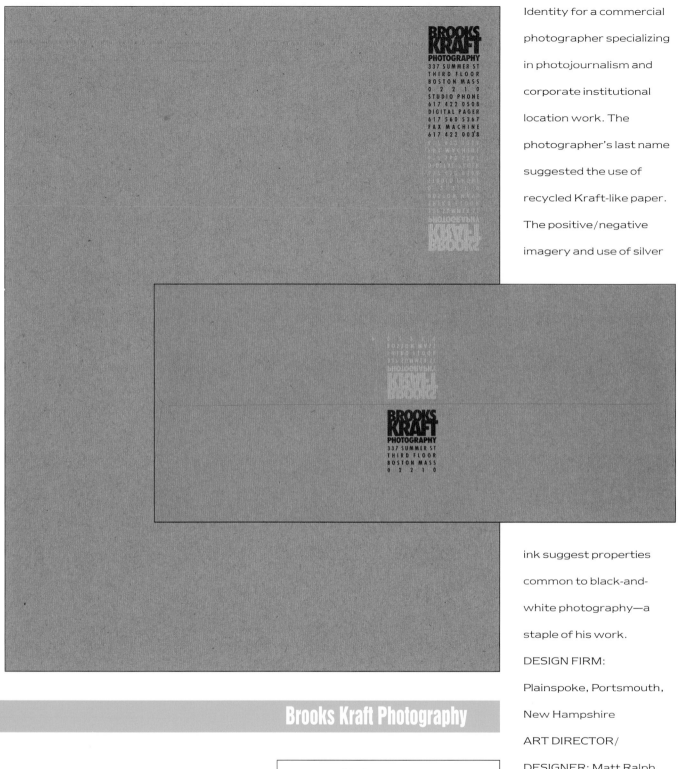

Identity for a commercial photographer specializing in photojournalism and corporate institutional location work. The photographer's last name suggested the use of recycled Kraft-like paper. The positive/negative imagery and use of silver ink suggest properties common to black-and-white photography—a staple of his work.

DESIGN FIRM: Plainspoke, Portsmouth, New Hampshire

ART DIRECTOR/ DESIGNER: Matt Ralph

BUDGET: Printing: $975

PRINTING PROCESS: 2-color (black and metallic silver), offset

Brooks Kraft Photography

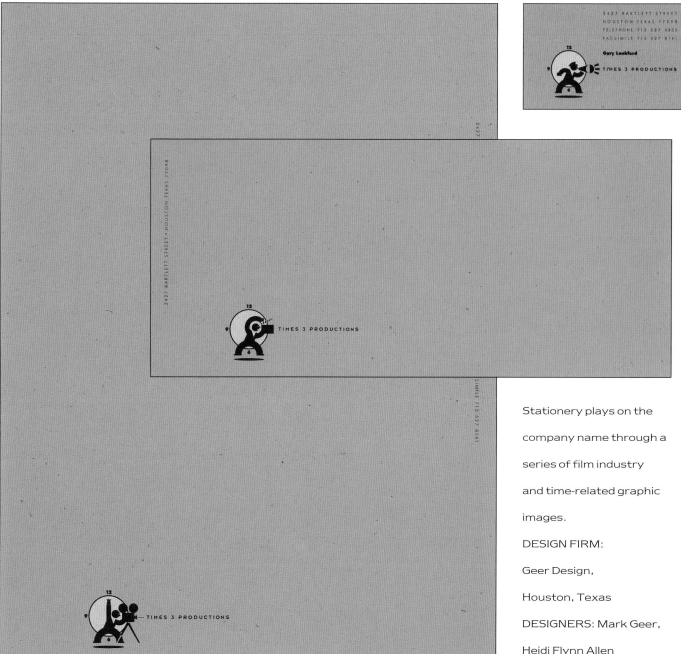

2427 BARTLETT STREET
HOUSTON TEXAS 77098
TELEPHONE 713 527 0333
FACSIMILE 713 527 8141

Gary Lankford

TIMES 3 PRODUCTIONS

Stationery plays on the company name through a series of film industry and time-related graphic images.

DESIGN FIRM: Geer Design, Houston, Texas

DESIGNERS: Mark Geer, Heidi Flynn Allen

PRINTING PROCESS: 2-color (opaque white and dry-trap black), offset

Times 3 Productions (Film Production)

Notecard.

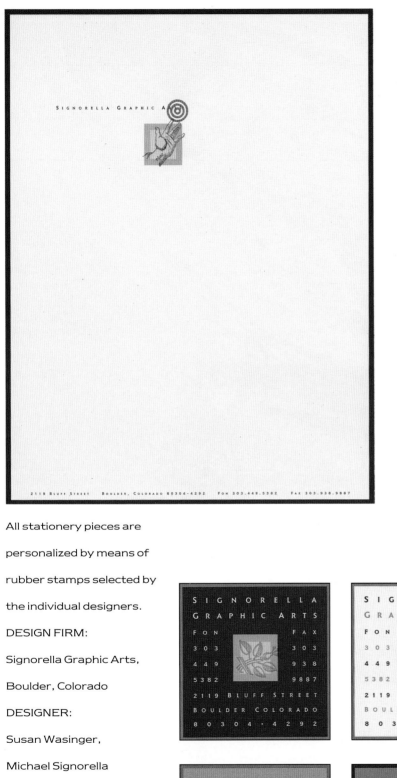

All stationery pieces are personalized by means of rubber stamps selected by the individual designers.

DESIGN FIRM:

Signorella Graphic Arts, Boulder, Colorado

DESIGNER:

Susan Wasinger, Michael Signorella

PRINTER: D+K Printing, Inc.

BUDGET: Printing: $2000

PRINTING PROCESS:

3-colors (PMS) in different combinations

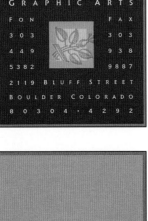

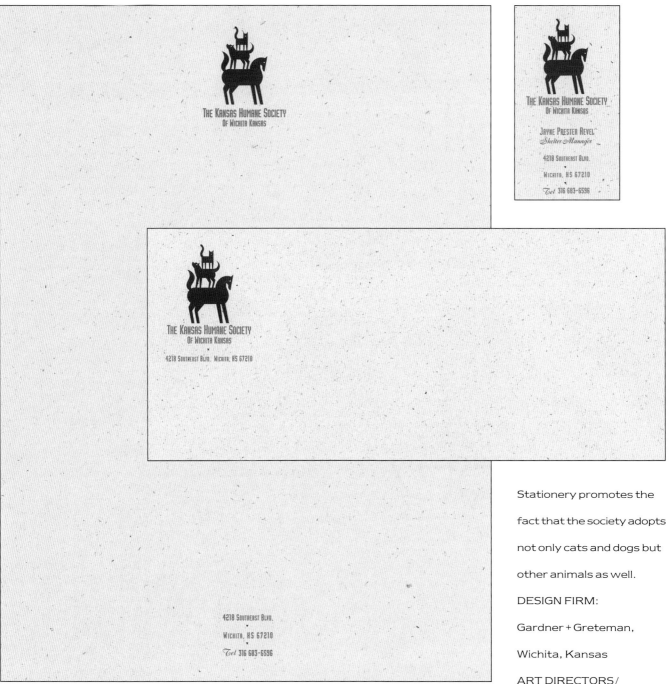

Certificate.

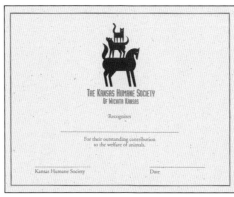

Stationery promotes the fact that the society adopts not only cats and dogs but other animals as well.

DESIGN FIRM:

Gardner + Greteman, Wichita, Kansas

ART DIRECTORS/

DESIGNERS: Sonia Greteman, Bill Gardner

ILLUSTRATOR:

Mike Kastens

BUDGET: Design: $1000; printing: $500

PRINTING PROCESS:

2 PMS flats

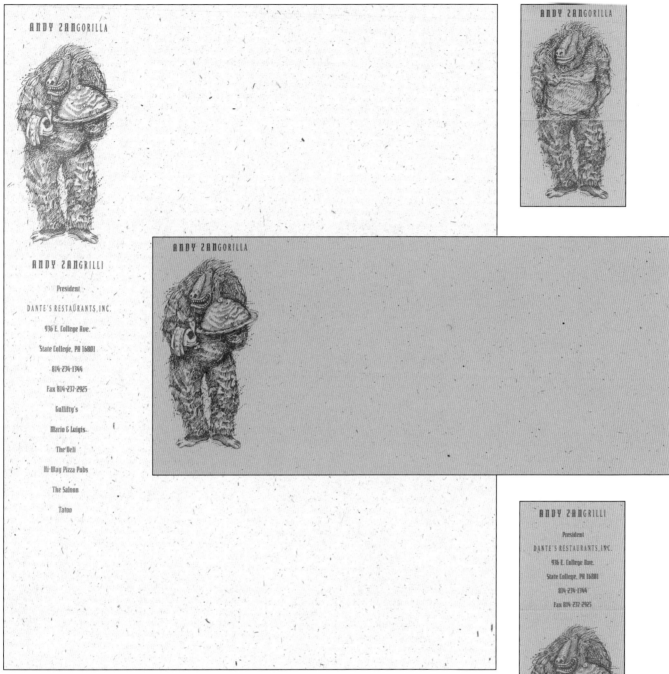

Design is inspired by the company president's nickname—Andy Zangorilla. He has a hands-on approach and wanted to be perceived as personable. The images are updated as the list of his restaurants changes.

DESIGN FIRM:

Sommese Design, State College, Pennsylvania

ART DIRECTORS:

Kristin and Lanny Sommese

DESIGNER:

Kristin Sommese

ILLUSTRATOR:

Lanny Sommese

BUDGET: $550

PRINTING PROCESS:

Offset lithography

Business card folded (top) and unfolded (above).

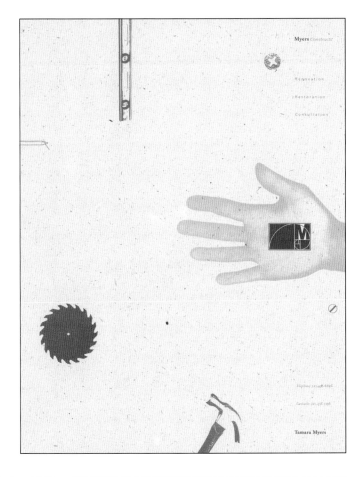

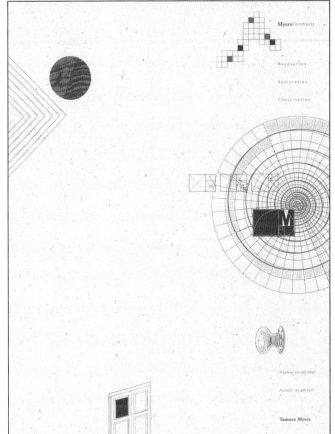

This small firm redirected its marketing effort to target subcontractors of high-end custom carpentry and construction. Augmenting the firm's standard letterhead, three custom letterheads aimed at architects, interior designers and large-scale construction companies were created for a quarterly mailing in lieu of a brochure.

DESIGN FIRM:
Bjornson Design
Associates, Inc.,
Philadelphia, Pennsylvania
ART DIRECTOR/
DESIGNER:
Jon Anders Bjornson
BUDGET: Design: $3000
(taken in trade—client
built Bjornson's kitchen);
printing: $3000
PRINTING PROCESS:
All images photocopied;
3-color, offset; custom
letterheads gang printed
with standard letterhead.

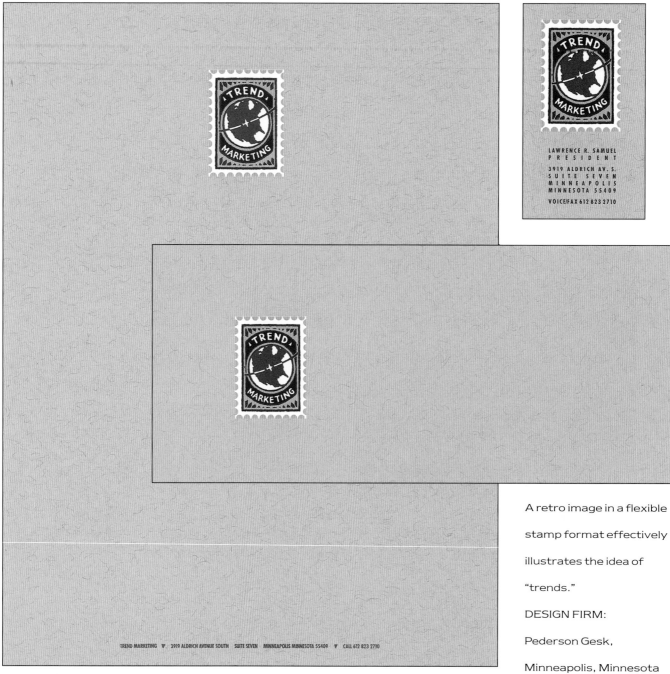

LAWRENCE R. SAMUEL
P R E S I D E N T
3919 ALDRICH AV. S.
S U I T E S E V E N
M I N N E A P O L I S
M I N N E S O T A 5 5 4 0 9
VOICE/FAX 612 823 2710

TREND MARKETING ▼ 3919 ALDRICH AVENUE SOUTH   SUITE SEVEN   MINNEAPOLIS MINNESOTA 55409   ▼   CALL 612 823 2710

Trend Marketing (Trend Consulting)

A retro image in a flexible stamp format effectively illustrates the idea of "trends."

DESIGN FIRM:
Pederson Gesk,
Minneapolis, Minnesota
DESIGNER/ILLUSTRATOR:
Mitchell Lindgren
BUDGET: Design and
production: $4000;
printing: $2000
PRINTING PROCESS:
1-color (paper stock),
3-color (stamp)

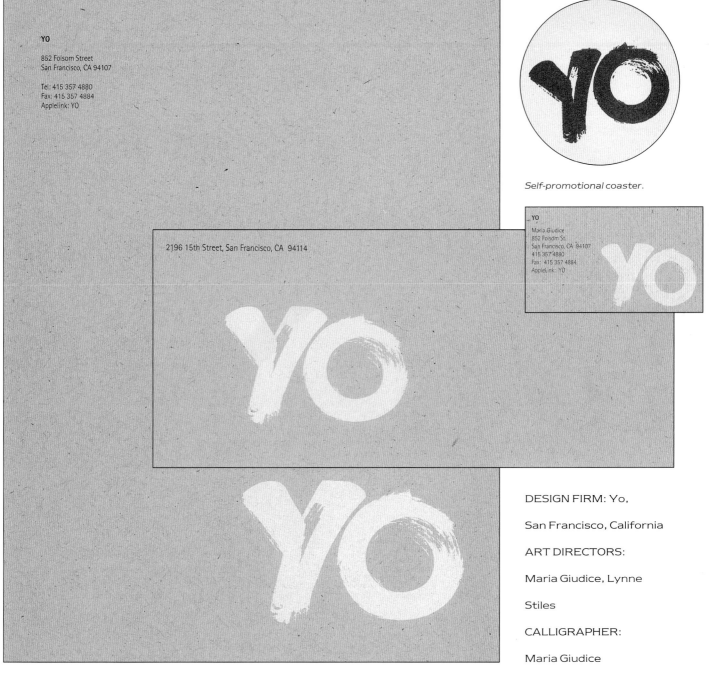

YO

852 Folsom Street
San Francisco, CA 94107

Tel: 415 357 4880
Fax: 415 357 4884
Applelink: YO

2196 15th Street, San Francisco, CA 94114

Self-promotional coaster.

YO
Maria Giudice
852 Folsom St.
San Francisco, CA 94107
415 357 4880
Fax: 415 357 4884
AppleLink: YO

Yo (Publication and Information Design)

DESIGN FIRM: Yo,
San Francisco, California
ART DIRECTORS:
Maria Giudice, Lynne
Stiles
CALLIGRAPHER:
Maria Giudice
BUDGET: Printing: $800
(stationery, business
cards)
PRINTING PROCESS:
Black + triple hit white ink,
offset lithography
PAPER: French
Speckletone oatmeal

*Christmas card (left) sent
during Yo's first year of
business.*

HO HO YO!

Holiday greetings from YO,
the new design partnership of
Maria Giudice and Lynne Stiles.

Front and back of letterhead.

Front and back of business card.

The package establishes

a corporate identity with

a lively interactive look

and feel.

DESIGN FIRM:

Tharp Did It, Los Gatos,

California

ART DIRECTOR:

Rick Tharp

DESIGNERS: Rick Tharp,

Jean Mogannam

PRINTING PROCESS:

3-color, offset

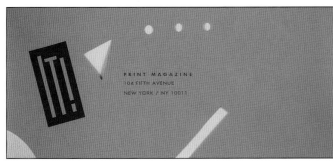

Julio Lima's Cuban heritage and extensive experience in the Caribbean and Latin America influenced his choice of a rainbow of bright tropical colors for his stationery. Each envelope is custom die-cut by hand, allowing the letterhead color to show through.

DESIGN FIRM: IT!, Orlando, Florida

DESIGNER: Julio Lima

BUDGET: Paper: $30 per 500 sheets

PRINTING PROCESS: Laser printed in black

The designer came up with the company name and designed the luggage-label-looking stationery to evoke exotic travel.

DESIGN FIRM:

Paramount Press, Brunswick, Georgia

ART DIRECTOR/ DESIGNER:

Barbara Ingram

PRODUCTION:

Paramount Press

BUDGET: Design: $1200; printing: $500

PRINTING PROCESS:

3 PMS spot colors on recycled stock

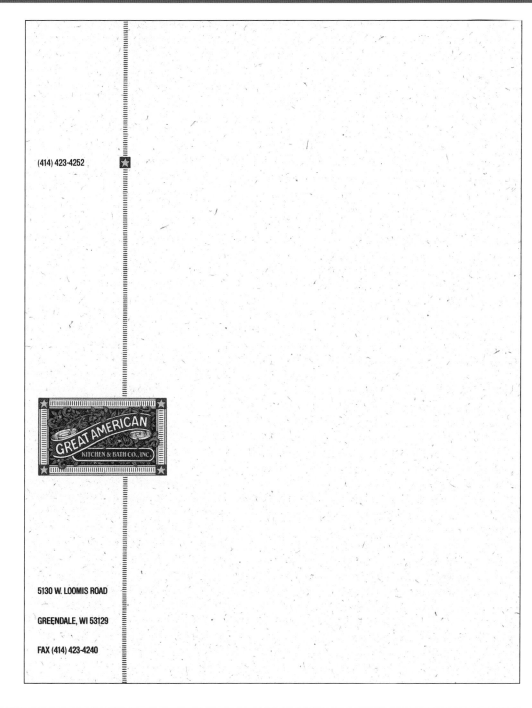

(414) 423-4252

5130 W. LOOMIS ROAD

GREENDALE, WI 53129

FAX (414) 423-4240

5130 W. LOOMIS ROAD

GREENDALE, WI 53129

This letterhead for designers of kitchens and baths in decorative, early-American style is meant to evoke a friendly, down-home approach to business and service.

DESIGN FIRM: Mydlach Design, Milwaukee, Wisconsin

ART DIRECTOR/ DESIGNER: Karen Mydlach

ILLUSTRATOR: Renée Graef

PRINTER: Heritage Printing

BUDGET: Design, illustration and production: $3000; printing: $3500 for 10,000 business cards, 5000 envelopes, 5000 letterheads

PRINTING PROCESS: 2-color press (Ryobi 3302)

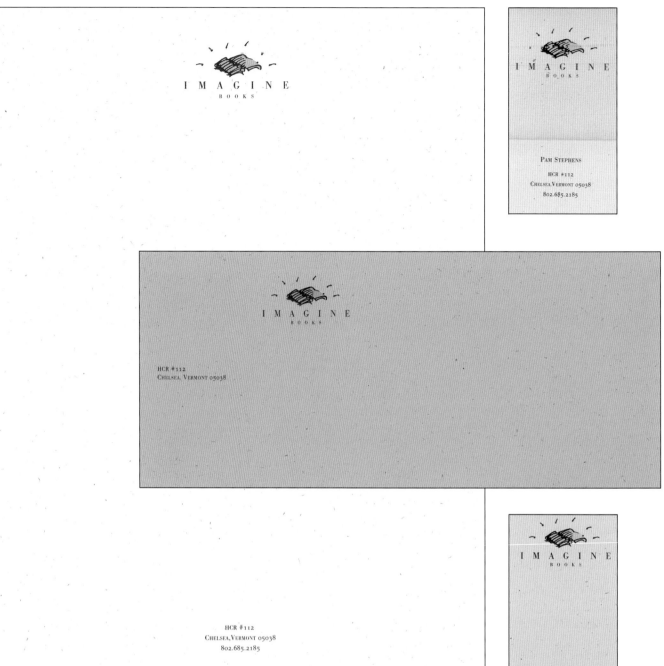

Imagine Books

Dealer in first-edition and antique collectible books.

DESIGN FIRM:

KAISERDICKEN, Burlington, Vermont

ART DIRECTOR/

DESIGNER: Debra Kaiser

ILLUSTRATOR:

Craig Dicken

BUDGET: Design: annual payments based on longevity of logo; printing: $850 (printer donated the opaque inks and an

additional hit on the yellow)

PRINTING PROCESS:

Black + separate opaque PMS for each piece

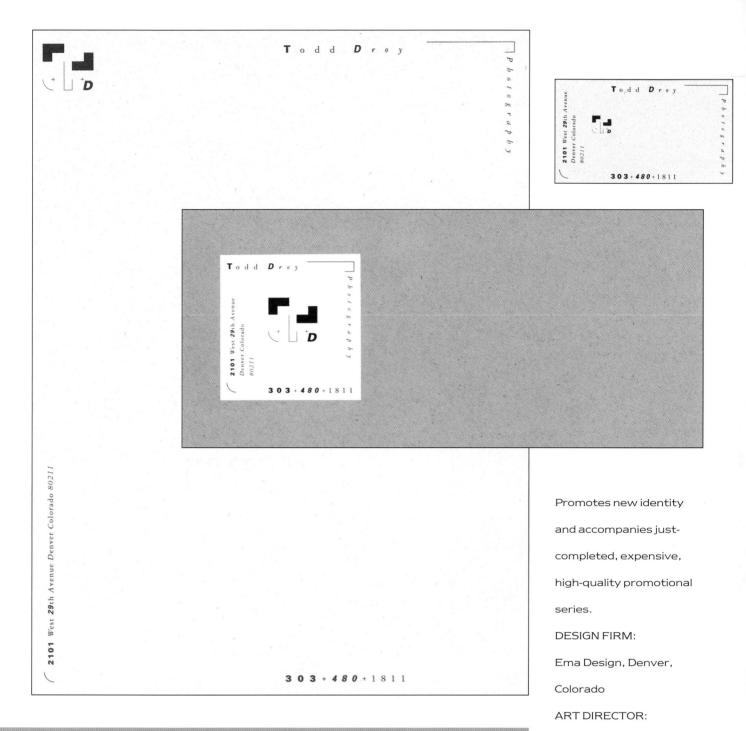

Promotes new identity and accompanies just-completed, expensive, high-quality promotional series.

DESIGN FIRM:

Ema Design, Denver, Colorado

ART DIRECTOR:

Thomas C. Ema

DESIGNER:

Debra Johnson Humphrey

BUDGET: $1000

PRINTING PROCESS:

1-color (black) offset

Todd Droy Photography

AH! LA FAX
FROM DESIGN AH! LA FINE
FAX: 310. 379. 2267

DATE:

COMPANY:

ATTN:

RE:

PAGES:

MESSAGE:

DESIGN FIRM:

Design Ah! La Fine,

Manhattan Beach,

California

ART DIRECTOR:

Andrea Micallef

DESIGNER: Al Grellmann

PRINTING PROCESS:

Laser output

Design Ah! La Fine (Graphic Design)

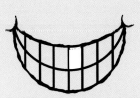

Gus Thompson, Hockey Coach

Stationery promotes a
volunteer coach for an
inner city hockey league.
DESIGN FIRM:
Odney Advertising,
Minneapolis, Minnesota
ART DIRECTOR:
Chris Lincoln
BUDGET: Printing: $100
PRINTING PROCESS:
Black ink on text paper,
hand cut.

1935 Bayard Avenue St. Paul, MN 55116 · (612) 590-5131

Gus Thompson

Stationery depicts interactive media with all of its layers and movement.

DESIGN FIRM:

Stoltze Design, Boston, Massachusetts

ART DIRECTOR:

Clifford Stoltze

DESIGNERS: Peter Farrell, Clifford Stoltze

BUDGET: Design: $3000; printing: trade between Planet Interactive and the printer.

PRINTING PROCESS:

Offset with 4 PMS colors

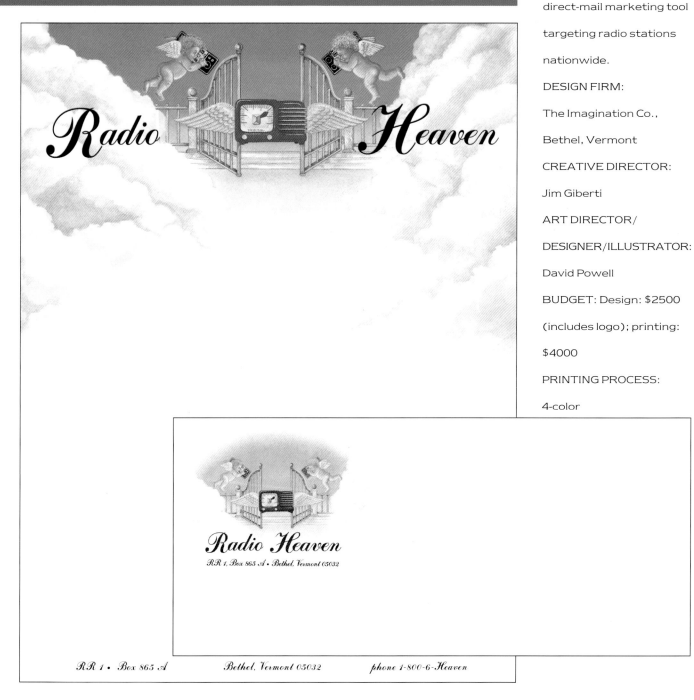

Stationery serves as a direct-mail marketing tool targeting radio stations nationwide.

DESIGN FIRM:

The Imagination Co., Bethel, Vermont

CREATIVE DIRECTOR:

Jim Giberti

ART DIRECTOR/ DESIGNER/ILLUSTRATOR:

David Powell

BUDGET: Design: $2500 (includes logo); printing: $4000

PRINTING PROCESS:

4-color

Envirographics (Mapping)

Map-making symbols depict the firm's field of endeavor.

DESIGN FIRM:

Peter Good Graphic

Design, Chester,

Connecticut

ART DIRECTOR/

DESIGNER/ILLUSTRATOR:

Peter Good

COMPUTER GRAPHICS:

Ed Kim

PRINTING PROCESS:

Offset

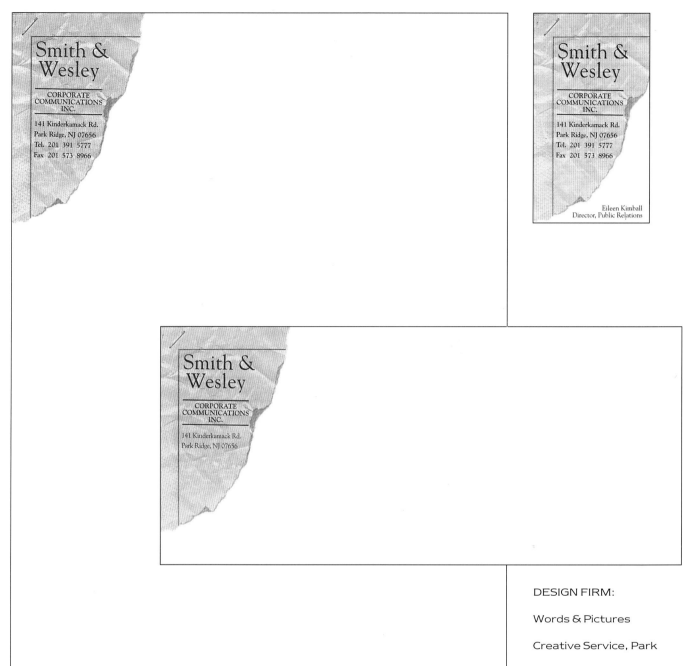

Smith & Wesley Corporate Communications (Public Relations)

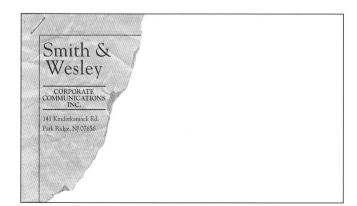

DESIGN FIRM:

Words & Pictures

Creative Service, Park

Ridge, New Jersey

ART DIRECTOR:

Wesley Shaw

DESIGNERS:

Smita Aggarwal, Angela

Vario

BUDGET: $1500

PRINTING PROCESS:

2-color

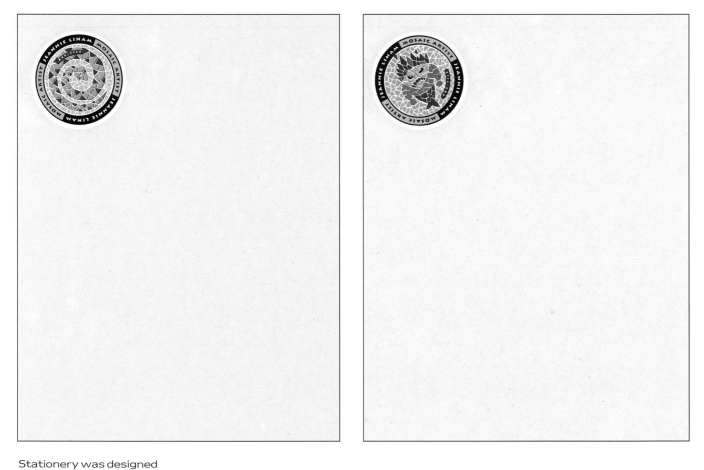

Stationery was designed
to establish Linam and
separate her from the
competition.

DESIGN FIRM:
Pennebaker Design,
Houston, Texas
ART DIRECTOR/
DESIGNER: Jeffrey McKay
BUDGET: $750 and
tradeout for table design
for design firm's
conference room.
PRINTING PROCESS:
4-color and thermography

On a low budget, stickers offered a variety of paper stock options. The designer took his wife's family name because his name, Gyongy, is difficult to pronounce.

DESIGNER: Roy Fox, Hollis, Maine

FILM SEPARATIONS: Imageset, Portland, Maine

PRINTING PROCESS: 3-color on off-white adhesive stock

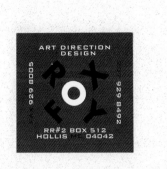

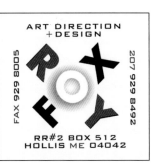

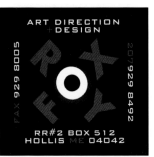

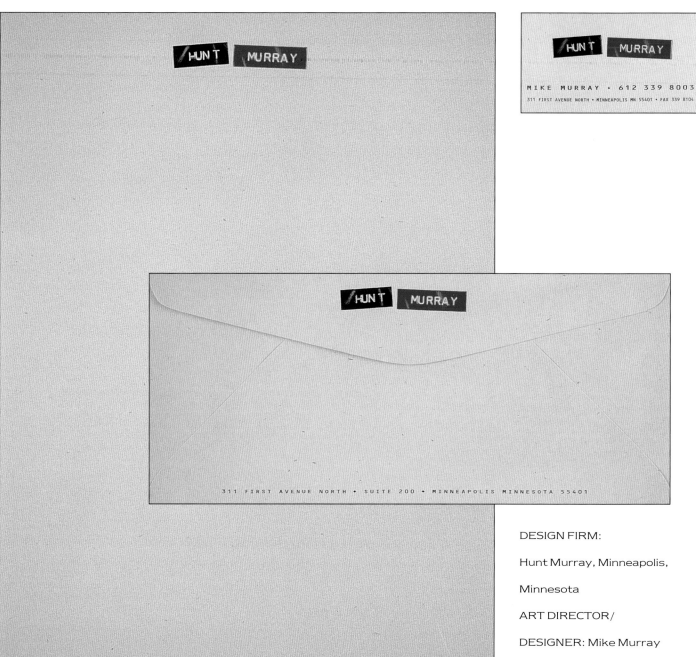

DESIGN FIRM:

Hunt Murray, Minneapolis,

Minnesota

ART DIRECTOR/

DESIGNER: Mike Murray

PRINTING PROCESS:

2-color lithography,

embossed with two foils

Hunt Murray (Advertising/Design)

The symbol for a healthcare ad agency's special project division depicts its video capabilities combined with written proposal skills. The image forms a caduceus, symbol of medicine.

DESIGN FIRM:

Cline, Davis & Mann, Inc., New York, New York

ART DIRECTOR:

Andy Moore

ILLUSTRATOR:

Eskil Ohlsson

MANAGING DIRECTOR:

Phillip Roselin

PRINTING PROCESS:

2-color

TEXAS ORTHOPEDIC HOSPITAL
A Specialty Surgery, Rehabilitation and Sports Medicine Center

TEXAS ORTHOPEDIC HOSPITAL
A Specialty Surgery, Rehabilitation and
Sports Medicine Center

Kathy Sunderland
Administrative Assistant

7515 S. Main Street
Suite 290
Houston, TX 77030
713 799 8600
Fax 713 799 1827

TEXAS ORTHOPEDIC HOSPITAL
A Specialty Surgery, Rehabilitation and Sports Medicine Center

7515 S. Main Street, Suite 290 Houston, TX 77030 713.799.8600 Fax 713.799.1827
An affiliate of Columbia Healthcare Corporation

Texas Orthopedic Hospital

Package presents a

contemporary image for a

newly-built orthopedic

hospital.

DESIGN FIRM:

Pennebaker Design,

Houston, Texas

ART DIRECTOR/

DESIGNER:

Haesun Kim Lerch

BUDGET: $6500

PRINTING PROCESS:

4-color

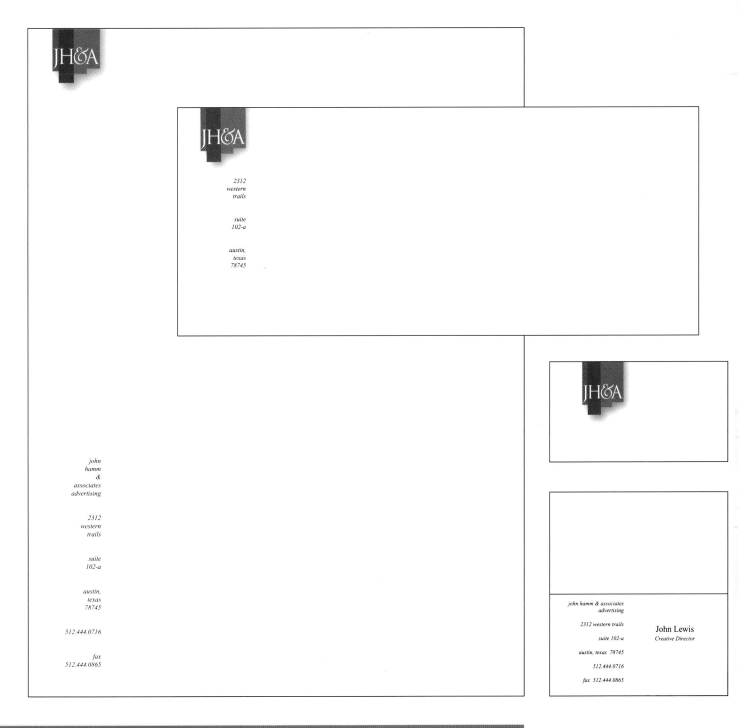

2312
western
trails

suite
102-a

austin,
texas
78745

john
hamm
&
associates
advertising

2312
western
trails

suite
102-a

austin,
texas
78745

512.444.0716

fax
512.444.0865

john hamm & associates
advertising

2312 western trails

suite 102-a

austin, texas 78745

512.444.0716

fax 512.444.0865

John Lewis
Creative Director

JH&A Advertising (Advertising/Marketing)

Package is part of an overall identity program promoting the firm's new name, logo, and corporate direction.

DESIGN FIRM:

JH&A Advertising, Austin, Texas

ART DIRECTOR/

DESIGNER: John Lewis

COMPUTER PRODUCTION:

Bryan Bassett

PRINTING PROCESS:

4-color

91

Reneé Williams
Illustrator
537
Stahr Road.
Apartment #1,
Elkins Park, PA
19117

215.635.4142

Different characters link the individual cards in the series to the illustrator's letterhead.

ART DIRECTOR/ DESIGNER/ILLUSTRATOR: Reneé Williams

BUDGET: Printing: $40 (photocopying), $120 (stock)

PRINTING PROCESS: Photocopy. Pen and ink drawings and lettering

Reneé Williams

This graphic illustration/ logo instantly calls up the name of the studio and its principal. With the birth of Hynson's son, the stationery now serves as personal stationery as well.

(hen)•(son)

robert hynson
3911 overlea avenue
baltimore, maryland 21206

robert hynson • 3911 overlea avenue • baltimore, maryland 21206 • 410. 444. 6956

DESIGN FIRM:

Hynson Design,

Baltimore, Maryland

ART DIRECTOR/

DESIGNER: Bob Hynson

ILLUSTRATOR:

Scott Mattern

BUDGET: Design: $250;

printing: $500

PRINTING PROCESS:

4 PMS match colors

printed offset

Hynson Design (Advertising/Design)

(hen)•(son)

robert hynson

3911 overlea avenue
baltimore, maryland 21206
410. 444. 6956

River City Brewing Company

545 Downtown Plaza
Suite 1115
Krista Pereira
Sacramento, CA 95814
Tel 916.447.BREW

RIVER CITY BREWING COMPANY

This card introduces the largest micro-brewery in Sacramento as a fun place to go. An oversized card is handed out at the restaurant as a small ad. The client's favorite tag line for his place: "The hippest hops in town."

DESIGN FIRM:

The Dunlavey Studio, Inc., Sacramento, California

ART DIRECTOR:

Michael Dunlavey

DESIGNER/ILLUSTRATOR:

Lindy Dunlavey

BUDGET: Design: $3500; printing: $1100

PRINTING PROCESS:

4-color (PMS spot color with blends) offset

DESIGN FIRM:

Giles Design, San Antonio, Texas

ART DIRECTOR: Jill Giles

DESIGNERS:

Cindy Greenwood,

Barbara Schelling,

Deborah Sweet

PRINTING PROCESS:

PMS spot color (3 colors)

Sprott Nichols Design (Interior Design)

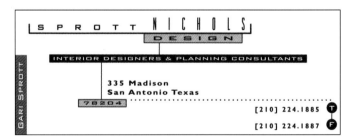

SPROTT NICHOLS DESIGN

INTERIOR DESIGNERS & PLANNING CONSULTANTS

GARI SPROTT

335 Madison
San Antonio Texas

78204

[210] 224.1885 T
[210] 224.1887 F

Segura Inc. (Graphic Design)

SEGURA 361 WEST CHESTNUT STREET, FIRST FLOOR, CHICAGO, ILLINOIS 60610, USA. TEL 312.649.5688, FAX 312.649.0376, CEL 312.316.3664

DESIGN FIRM: Segura Inc, Chicago, Illinois

ART DIRECTOR/ DESIGNER: Carlos Segura

PHOTOGRAPHER:

Greg Heck

BUDGET: $3000 for 2000 cards

PRINTING PROCESS:

4-color (front), 1-color (back)

WATCH CHILDREN

Cynthia Thomassey

Child Care, Day Care, Babysitting

286 Brighton Street
East Pittsburgh, PA 15112

412 824-2992

The idea here is that once you've seen this business card, it would be hard to pass the familiar traffic icon without being reminded of Thomassey's childcare service.
DESIGN FIRM:
Seman Design,
Pittsburgh, Pennsylvania

ART DIRECTOR/
DESIGNER:
Richard M. Seman
ILLUSTRATOR:
Doug Freeman
BUDGET: Design bartered for childcare services; printing: $75
PRINTING PROCESS:
2-color offset with thermography on both colors.

Cynthia Thomassey (Childcare)

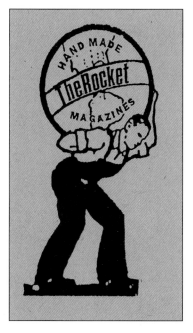

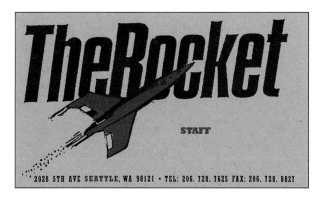

Staff business card for a twice-monthly music and related culture magazine.
ART DIRECTOR/
DESIGNER:
Jeff Kelinsmith/The Rocket Magazine,
Seattle, Washington
BUDGET: Design: in-house; printing: $400
PRINTING PROCESS:
2-color front (black/PMS red), 1-color back (black)

The Rocket Magazine

ABBY E. HERGET
26 JULIUS STREET, SAN FRANCISCO, CA 94133
415.982.4437

DESIGN FIRM:

Burson-Marsteller,

San Francisco, California

ART DIRECTOR/

DESIGNER/ILLUSTRATOR:

Abby E. Herget

PRINTING PROCESS:

1-color, offset lithography;

large A is cut with pinking

shears from paper scraps,

then sewn on with buttons.

ABBY E. HERGET
26 JULIUS STREET, SAN FRANCISCO, CA 94133
415.982.4437

ABBY E. HERGET
26 JULIUS STREET, SAN FRANCISCO, CA 94133
415.982.4437

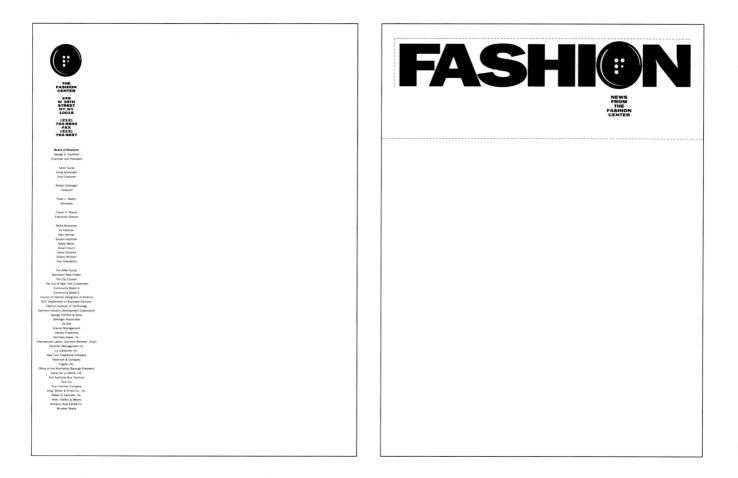

The Fashion Center

The Fashion Center is a business improvement district formed by property owners in midtown Manhattan who wish to take an active role in bettering their neighborhood. The logo with its whimsical button establishes an identity for the organization, which represents the fashion/garment industry.

DESIGN FIRM:

Pentagram Design,

New York, New York

ART DIRECTORS:

Michael Bierut, Paula Scher

DESIGNER:

Esther Bridavsky

PRINTING PROCESS:

Offset

H _Haygeman_

Design
as it applies to
Marketing

2260 Rutherford Road
Suite 110
Carlsbad, CA 92008
619/931-1982
Fax 619/931-9096

I _Isobe_

2260 Rutherford Road
Suite 110
Carlsbad, CA 92008

J _Johnson_

H _Haygeman_   I _Isobe_   J _Johnson_   K _Kracke_

K _Kracke_

DESIGN FIRM: HIJK,

Carlsbad, California

ART DIRECTOR:

Drew Haygeman

DESIGNER: Craig Isobe

PRINTER: Full Court Press

BUDGET: Design: $5000;

CRA/printing: $7500

PRINTING PROCESS:

5 PMS colors, embossing

on recycled stock

HIJK (Graphic Design for Marketing)

Design
as it applies to
Marketing

Drew Haygeman

2260 Rutherford Road
Suite 110
Carlsbad, CA 92008
619/931-1982
Fax 619/931-9096

HIJK

Erika Reade Ltd.

Erika Reade Ltd.
TO:

Erika Reade Ltd.
3718 ROSWELL ROAD, N.W. ATLANTA, GEORGIA 30342

3718 ROSWELL ROAD, N.W. ATLANTA, GEORGIA 30342 404.233.3857

DESIGN FIRM:

Shaw Design & Production,

Atlanta, Georgia

DESIGNER: Susan Shaw

CALLIGRAPHER:

Nancy Feinman

PRINTING PROCESS:

1-color, lithography

Erika Reade Ltd. (Gifts/Interior Accessories for the Home)

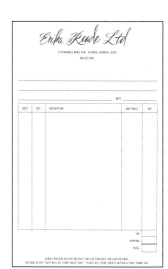

FIREWHEEL
AUTOMOTIVE

63 S. DEAN ST
ENGLEWOOD NJ
07631
TELEPHONE:
201 728 8665

FIREWHEEL   63 S. DEAN ST   TELEPHONE   Joseph A. Agresta, Jr.
AUTOMOTIVE   ENGLEWOOD   201 728 8665   *Vice President*
  NJ 07631

An innovative look helps a new company stand out from its considerable competition.

DESIGN FIRM:

David Morris Design Associates, Jersey City, New Jersey

ART DIRECTORS:

Timothy O'Donnell, David Annunziato

DESIGNER:

Timothy O'Donnell

BUDGET: Design: $3000; printing: $2000

PRINTING PROCESS:

Offset

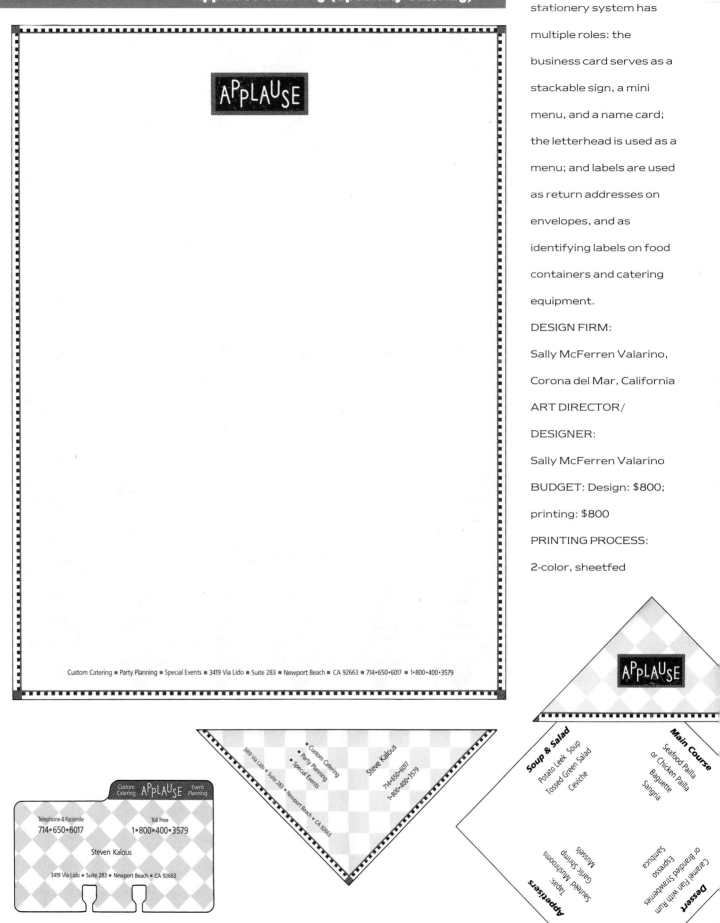

APPLAUSE

Custom Catering ▪ Party Planning ▪ Special Events ▪ 3419 Via Lido ▪ Suite 283 ▪ Newport Beach ▪ CA 92663 ▪ 714▪650▪6017 ▪ 1▪800▪400▪3579

Each piece in this stationery system has multiple roles: the business card serves as a stackable sign, a mini menu, and a name card; the letterhead is used as a menu; and labels are used as return addresses on envelopes, and as identifying labels on food containers and catering equipment.

DESIGN FIRM:

Sally McFerren Valarino, Corona del Mar, California

ART DIRECTOR/

DESIGNER:

Sally McFerren Valarino

BUDGET: Design: $800;

printing: $800

PRINTING PROCESS:

2-color, sheetfed

Custom Catering — APPLAUSE — Event Planning

Telephone & Facsimile
714▪650▪6017

Toll Free
1▪800▪400▪3579

Steven Kalous

3419 Via Lido ▪ Suite 283 ▪ Newport Beach ▪ CA 92663

3419 Via Lido ▪ Suite 283 ▪ Newport Beach ▪ CA 92663

▪ Custom Catering
▪ Party Planning
▪ Special Events

Steve Kalous

714▪650▪6017
1▪800▪400▪3579

APPLAUSE

Soup & Salad
Potato Leek Soup
Tossed Green Salad
Ceviche

Main Course
Seafood Pailla
or Chicken Pailla
Baguette
Sangria

Appetisers
Tapas:
Sauteed Mushrooms
Garlic Shrimp
Mussels

Dessert
Caramel Flan with Rum
or Brandied Strawberries
Espresso
Sambuca

UNION STATION
Est. 1993
BREWERY

BRIAN FLAGG
EXECUTIVE CHEF

36 EXCHANGE TERRACE
PROVIDENCE, RHODE ISLAND 02903
401-274-BREW, FAX 401-831-2120

PUB MENU

36 EXCHANGE TERRACE
PROVIDENCE, RHODE ISLAND 02903
401-274-BREW, FAX 401-831-2120

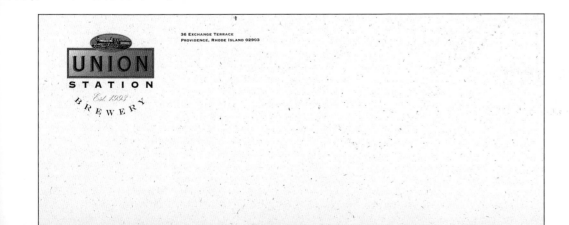

36 EXCHANGE TERRACE
PROVIDENCE, RHODE ISLAND 02903

MENU

UNION
STATION
Est. 1993
BREWERY

PROVIDENCE
RHODE ISLAND

There is currently an explosion of brew pubs and microbreweries. To cut through the clutter of new brands, the designers positioned Union Station Brewery as long established by giving it a vintage, historical look.

DESIGN FIRM: Adkins-Balchunas Design, Pawtucket, Rhode Island

ART DIRECTOR: Jerry Balchunas

DESIGNERS: Carl Bolton, Jerry Balchunas

BUDGET: Design: $5100; printing: $1200

PRINTING PROCESS: Offset

Union Station Brewery (Microbrewery/Brew Pub)

INTERNATIONAL INSTITUTE FOR THE HEALING OF RACISM

Route 113, Box 232
Thetford, VT 05074
802 785 2627
Fax 802 785 4969

540 Hinman
Suite 300
Evanston, IL 60202
708 492 0123

HEALING OF RACISM

Rita Starr

INTERNATIONAL INSTITUTE FOR THE

540 Hinman, Suite 300
Evanston, IL 60202
708 492 0123

HEALING OF RACISM

Humanity is one

Route 113, Box 232
Thetford, VT 05074

INTERNATIONAL INSTITUTE FOR THE

540 Hinman, Suite 300
Evanston, IL 60202

HEALING OF RACISM

Humanity is one

Humanity is one

The International Institute for the Healing of Racism

This package helped identify and establish the organization in its efforts to combat racism worldwide.

DESIGN FIRM:
Design Consortium,
Newburyport,
Massachusetts

ART DIRECTOR/
DESIGNER/ILLUSTRATOR:
Rose Russo

BUDGET: Design: pro bono;
printing: $2000

PRINTING PROCESS:
3-color, offset

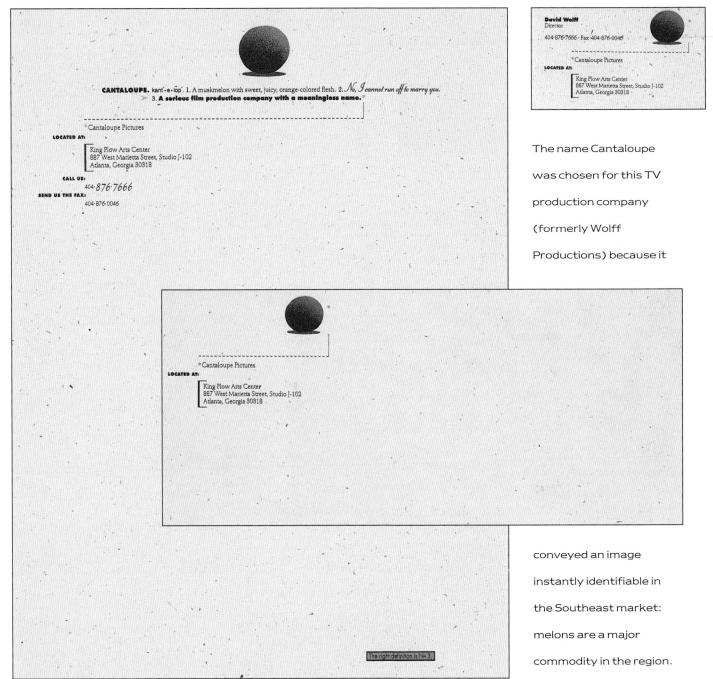

CANTALOUPE. kant´•e•lōp´. 1. A muskmelon with sweet, juicy, orange-colored flesh. 2. *No, I cannot run off to marry you.* > 3. **A serious film production company with a meaningless name.**

*Cantaloupe Pictures

LOCATED AT:

King Plow Arts Center
887 West Marietta Street, Studio J-102
Atlanta, Georgia 30318

CALL US:
404·876·7666

SEND US THE FAX:
404·876·0046

*Cantaloupe Pictures

LOCATED AT:

King Plow Arts Center
887 West Marietta Street, Studio J-102
Atlanta, Georgia 30318

The right definition is Nº 3.

David Wolff
Director
404·876·7666 · Fax·404·876·0046

*Cantaloupe Pictures

LOCATED AT:

King Plow Arts Center
887 West Marietta Street, Studio J-102
Atlanta, Georgia 30318

The name Cantaloupe was chosen for this TV production company (formerly Wolff Productions) because it conveyed an image instantly identifiable in the Southeast market: melons are a major commodity in the region.

DESIGN FIRM: Jane Hill Design, Atlanta, Georgia

DESIGNER: Jane Hill

PHOTOGRAPHER: David Wolff (melon)

BUDGET: Design: $750; printing: $1600

PRINTING PROCESS: 2-color, offset

Cantaloupe Pictures

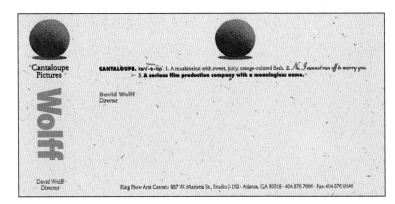

Cantaloupe Pictures

Wolff

David Wolff
Director

David Wolff
Director

CANTALOUPE. kant´•e•lōp´. 1. A muskmelon with sweet, juicy, orange-colored flesh. 2. *No, I cannot run off to marry you.* > 3. **A serious film production company with a meaningless name.**

David Wolff
Director   King Plow Arts Center· 887 W. Marietta St., Studio J-102 · Atlanta, GA 30318 · 404.876.7666 · Fax 404.876.0046

This first-of-its-kind retail audiology/hearing aid manufacturing lab wanted a letterhead that promoted the image of a stable, different, full-service business. The designers were involved in all phases of development including creating the name, which needed to be something friendly, not stuffy and clinical, as well as communicate a price-competitive position.

DESIGN FIRM:
The Puckett Group,
Atlanta, Georgia

ART DIRECTOR:
Kent Puckett

DESIGNER: Matt Smartt

BUDGET: Design: $15,000 (including development of name, logo, and applications); printing: $2000

PRINTING PROCESS:
3-color, offset

Phillip Parker

Photographer

385 South Main St.

Memphis, TN 38103

Tel (901)529-9200

Fax (901) 527-0353

Phillip Parker

Photographer

385 South Main St.

Memphis, TN 38103

Phillip Parker

Photographer

385 South Main St.

Memphis, TN 38103

Tel (901)529-9200

Fax (901) 527-0353

The end of a roll of film reinforces the *P* in Parker's first and last names and forms a simple, strong image that instantly identifies him to art directors and designers.

DESIGN FIRM: Disciple Design & Advertising, Memphis, Tennessee

ART DIRECTOR/ DESIGNER: Craig Thompson

ILLUSTRATORS: Craig Thompson, David Terry

BUDGET: Design/printing: in trade for photography services

PRINTING PROCESS: 2-color (black and warm gray), offset on light gray stock

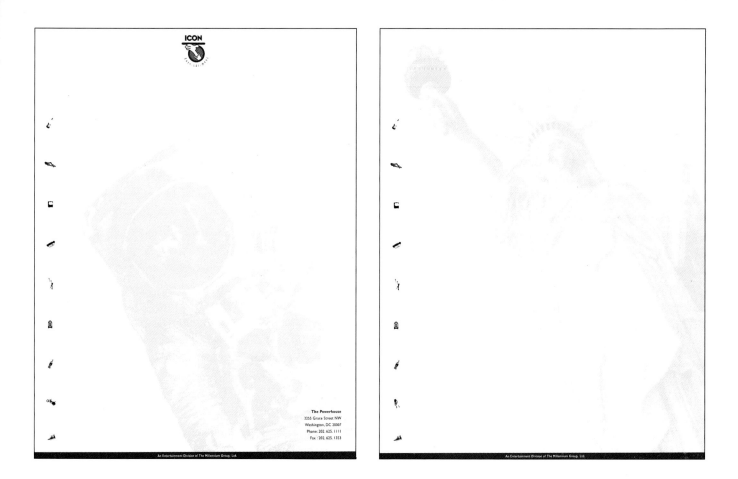

ICON

The Powerhouse
3255 Grace Street NW
Washington, DC 20007
Phone: 202. 625. 1111
Fax : 202. 625. 1353

An Entertainment Division of The Millennium Group, Ltd.

Icon Entertainment (Restaurant/Entertainment Management)

Back of all stationery.

ICON
Entertainment

The Powerhouse
3255 Grace Street, NW
Washington, DC 20007
Phone: 202. 625. 1111
Fax: 202. 625. 1353

Basel Dalloul
Chairman

An Entertainment Division of The Millennium Group, Ltd.

ICON
Entertainment

The Powerhouse
3255 Grace Street, NW
Washington, DC 20007
Phone: 202. 625. 1111
Fax: 202. 625. 1353

Doug Nunes
Staff Assistant

An Entertainment Division of The Millennium Group, Ltd.

ICON
Entertainment

The Powerhouse
3255 Grace Street NW
Washington, DC 20007

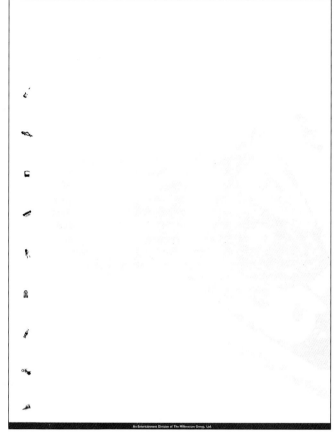

An identity that relied on iconography seemed apt for this project, so the designers conducted a search of American icons before narrowing the field to ten. Nine icons were placed along the left margin of the stationery and the remaining one was printed large across the body of the page, screened to 10 per cent. Different color combinations were chosen to set off the imagery.

DESIGN FIRM:
Magnet Design &
Communications,
Washington, DC
ART DIRECTORS:
Gregory R. Johnson,
Claudia Mejia
DESIGNERS:
Shane Brenizer,
Claudia Mejia
BUDGET: Design: $3200;
printing: $3000
PRINTING PROCESS:
2 PMS ; 1 PMS + varnish
(back of business card and
stationery)

Kid Marketing Group

DDB Needham Worldwide

BRAIN CHILD

303 East Wacker Drive, Chicago, Illinois 60601·5282   tel.312·861·0200   fax.312·552·2383

BRAIN CHILD
DDB Needham Worldwide

Kid Marketing Group

303 East Wacker Drive, Chicago, Illinois 60601·5282

Brain Child (Children's Product Marketing)

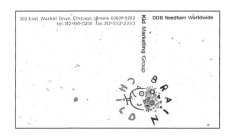

303 East Wacker Drive, Chicago, Illinois 60601·5282
tel.312·861·0200   fax.312·552·2383

Kid Marketing Group

DDB Needham Worldwide

BRAIN CHILD

DESIGN FIRM: Segura Inc.,

Chicago, Illinois

ART DIRECTOR:

Carlos Segura

DESIGNERS: Jon Stepping,

Carlos Segura

BUDGET: $4500 for 3000

letterheads and envelopes

PRINTING PROCESS:

3-color (front), 1-color

(back)

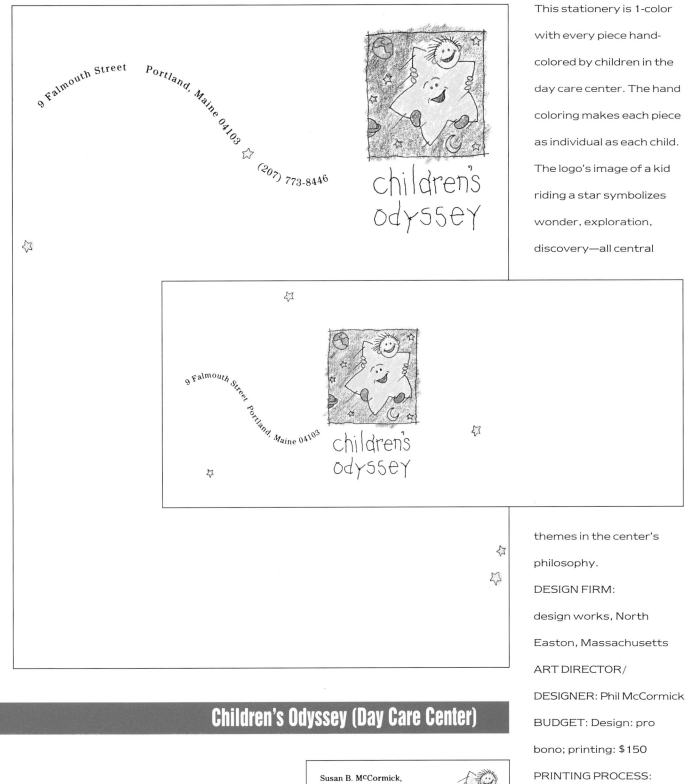

This stationery is 1-color with every piece hand-colored by children in the day care center. The hand coloring makes each piece as individual as each child. The logo's image of a kid riding a star symbolizes wonder, exploration, discovery—all central

themes in the center's philosophy.

DESIGN FIRM:
design works, North Easton, Massachusetts
ART DIRECTOR/
DESIGNER: Phil McCormick
BUDGET: Design: pro bono; printing: $150
PRINTING PROCESS:
1-color (black), offset

Children's Odyssey (Day Care Center)

FIRM: Design Center, Minnetonka, Minnesota
ART DIRECTOR: John Reger
DESIGNER: Todd Spichke
PRINTING PROCESS: 4 PMS colors were used for the cost of a 2-color job—gray, common to all pieces, plus one other color per piece.

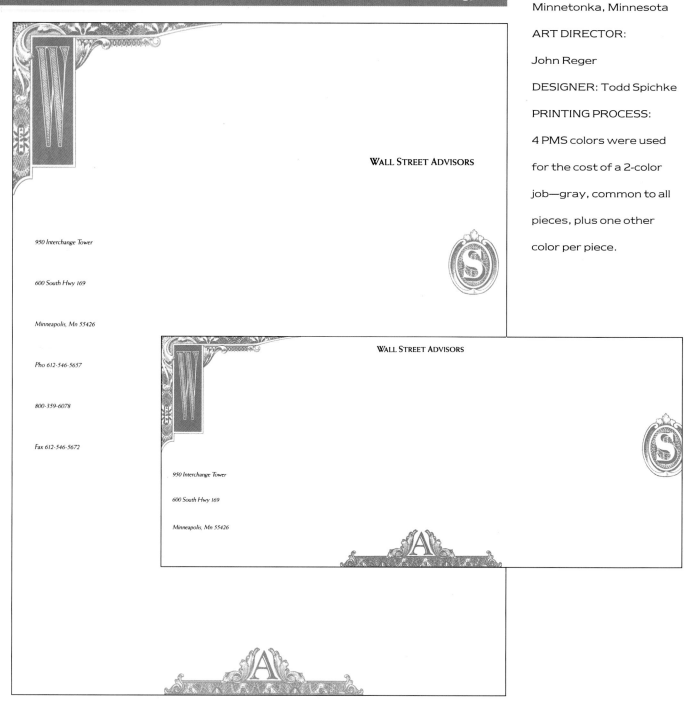

WALL STREET ADVISORS

950 Interchange Tower

600 South Hwy 169

Minneapolis, Mn 55426

Pho 612-546-5657

800-359-6078

Fax 612-546-5672

WALL STREET ADVISORS

950 Interchange Tower

600 South Hwy 169

Minneapolis, Mn 55426

Images of various environmental structures (buildings, bridges, archways) are used to announce the formation of a professional association for environmental designers.

DESIGN FIRM:
Skidmore, Owings & Merrill, San Francisco, California

ART DIRECTOR:
Lonny Israel

DESIGNERS:
Brad Thomas, Lonny Israel

BUDGET: Design: pro bono; printing: $500

PRINTING PROCESS:
1-color, offset

Environmental
DESIGN
Foundation

of Northern California

TRUSTEES
Margaret D. Woodring, President
Donald W. Bradley
Christopher C. Degenhardt
Nona B. Dennis
Charles N. Eley
Warren J. Hedgepeth
John L. Kriken
William W. Lee
Herbert E. Lembcke
Rosemary F. Muller
Michael J. Nilmeyer
Janet G. Roché
Robert B. Sena
Thomas B. Swift
Paul H. Sedway

ADVISORS
H. Grant Dehart
William D. Evers
Robert A. Odermatt
Paolo Polledri
George T. Rockrise
Richard E. Watson

EXECUTIVE DIRECTOR
James T. Chappell

130 Sutter Street
San Francisco, CA 94104
415 982 2151

Environmental
DESIGN
Foundation

of Northern California

130 Sutter Street
San Francisco, CA 94104

Environmental
DESIGN
Foundation

of Northern California

James T. Chappell
Executive Director

130 Sutter Street
San Francisco, CA 94104
415 982 2151

Environmental
DESIGN
Foundation

of Northern California

We acknowledge with pleasure your significant contribution to the preservation and enhancement of the quality of life in Northern California.

President   Date

113

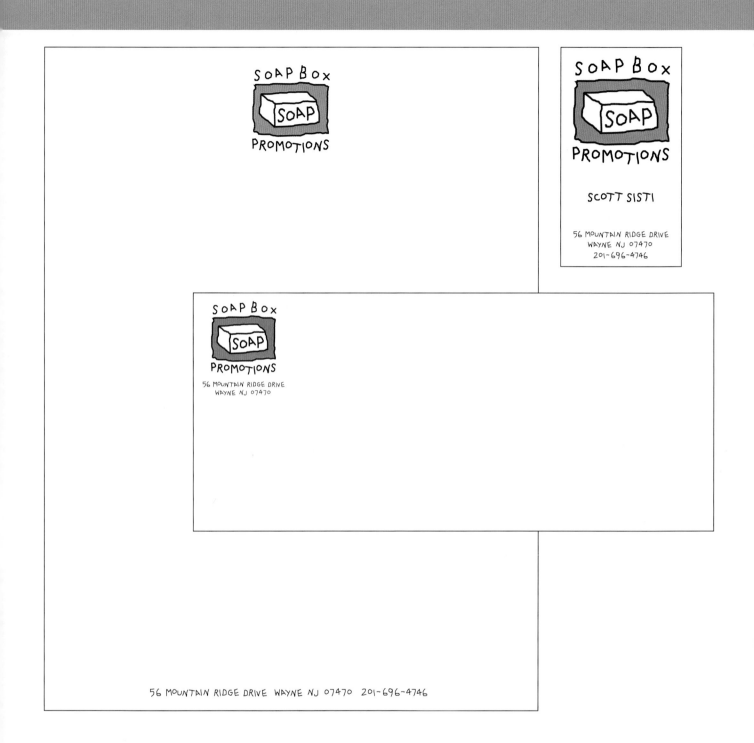

SOAP BOX
SOAP
PROMOTIONS

JUST A FEW FAX

1. ON THE AVERAGE, AMERICANS EAT 10 POUNDS OF CHOCOLATE PER YEAR

2. THE LARGEST WEIGHING APPENDIX REMOVED FROM A PATIENT WAS 13 LBS.

3.

| DATE | | TO | |
| PAGES | | FROM | |

56 MOUNTAIN RIDGE DRIVE WAYNE NJ 07470 201-696-4746

SOAP BOX
SOAP
PROMOTIONS

ALL WASHED UP

DATE	
INVOICE NUMBER	
CLIENT	
JOB NUMBER	
DESCRIPTION	
SUBTOTAL	
TAX	
AMOUNT DUE	

PLEASE MAKE CHECKS PAYABLE TO SOAPBOX PROMOTIONS · NET 30 DAYS · THANK YOU

56 MOUNTAIN RIDGE DRIVE WAYNE NJ 07470 201-696-4746

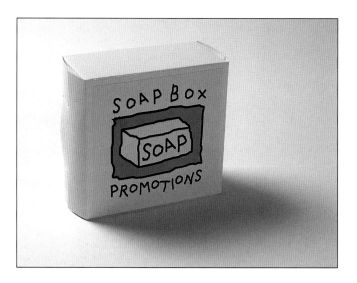

Corporate identity for a marketing/promotion firm. The stationery had to be flexible because business forms were designed to be printed on laserwriter on pre-printed letterheads.
DESIGN FIRM: Art Shop, Wayne, New Jersey

ART DIRECTOR/ DESIGNER: Carrie Sisti-Burns
BUDGET: Design: $1000; printing: $500
PRINTING PROCESS: 2-color (black + PMS), laserwriter on printed letterhead for business forms.

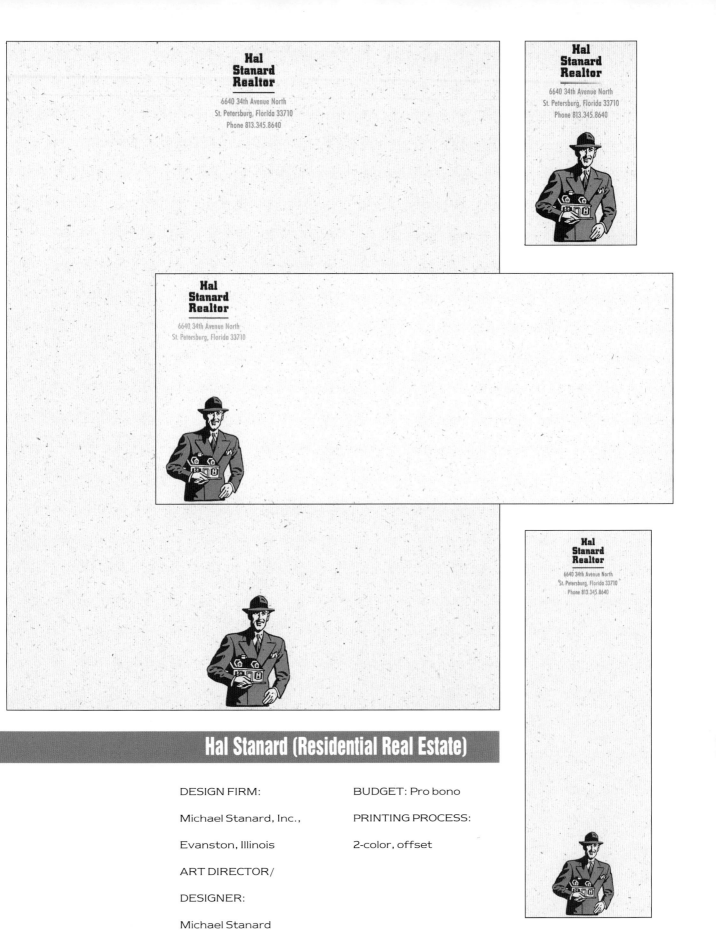

Hal Stanard (Residential Real Estate)

DESIGN FIRM:

Michael Stanard, Inc.,

Evanston, Illinois

ART DIRECTOR/

DESIGNER:

Michael Stanard

BUDGET: Pro bono

PRINTING PROCESS:

2-color, offset

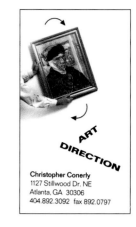

Christopher Conerly
1127 Stillwood Dr. NE
Atlanta, GA 30306
404.892.3092 fax 892.0797

Christopher Conerly
1127 Stillwood Dr. NE
Atlanta, GA 30306

Christopher Conerly
1127 Stillwood Dr. NE
Atlanta, GA 30306
404.892.3092 fax 892.0797

Christopher Conerly (Advertising/Independent Creative Director)

Christopher Conerly
1127 Stillwood Dr. NE
Atlanta, GA 30306
404.892.3092 fax 892.0797

This stationery was originally intended to be 4-color, but the designer felt the idea worked better in black-and-white.

DESIGN FIRM: Art Direction, Atlanta, Georgia

ART DIRECTOR/ DESIGNER: Christopher Conerly

PHOTOGRAPHER: Dave Shaffer

RETOUCHING: Danny Strickland

BUDGET: Photography: $35 (film and production only), $75 (retouching); printing: $250

PRINTING PROCESS: 1-color, offset

PAPER: Classic Crest

CREATIVE
·············
SEARCH
*

The identity for this
advertising/design
industry recruitment firm
evokes the company's
enthusiasm and appeals to
both client audiences—
design/advertising firms
and prospective job
candidates. To minimize
cost and maximize
flexibility, the 1994
stationery package was
created using four
different gummed
stamps, which add a sense
of immediacy and depict

CREATIVE
·············
SEARCH

113 Edinburgh South
Suite 203
Cary,
North Carolina
27511
Telephone
919 460 9595
Facsimile
919 460 0642
A Division of
Sales Consultants

113 Edinburgh South
Suite 203
Cary,
North Carolina
27511

CREATIVE
·············
SEARCH

113 Edinburgh South, Suite 203
Cary, North Carolina 27511
Facsimile 919 460 0642
A Division of Sales Consultants
MICHAEL PALMA
Busy Guy
Telephone 919 460 9595

Annual versions of stationery
include 1993 (this page) and
1994 (opposite page).

CREATIVE
·············
SEARCH

113 Edinburgh South, Suite 203
Cary, North Carolina 27511
Facsimile 919 460 0642
A Division of Sales Consultants
MICHAEL PALMA
Busy Guy
Telephone 919 460 9595

Café Voltaire
3231 North Clark Street Chicago, IL 60657 312-528-3136
handmade natural foods, theory, manifestoes, poems, pictures, music, performance, coffee

Treating the vegetables as the stars in this stationery package conveys the seriousness of the owner's vegetarian commitment.

DESIGN FIRM:

Rock, Paper, Scissors,

Chicago, Illinois

ART DIRECTORS/

DESIGNERS: Diane Purcell,

Steve Wall

PHOTOGRAPHER:

Gail Pollard

BUDGET: Design

(including photography

and prepress): $1500;

printing (including paper):

$3500

PAPER: Cross Pointe

Genesis (milkweed)

PRINTING PROCESS:

1-color, offset lithography

Café Voltaire
3231 North Clark Street Chicago, IL 60657 312-528-3136
handmade natural foods, theory, manifestoes, poems, pictures, music, performance, coffee

Café Voltaire (Vegetarian Restaurant/Coffee House/Theater)

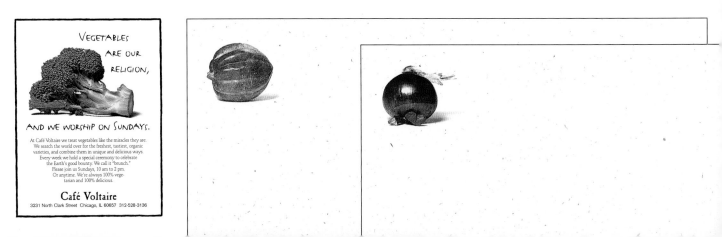

VEGETABLES ARE OUR RELIGION,

AND WE WORSHIP ON SUNDAYS.

At Café Voltaire we treat vegetables like the miracles they are. We search the world over for the freshest, tastiest, organic varieties, and combine them in unique and delicious ways. Every week we hold a special ceremony to celebrate the Earth's good bounty. We call it "brunch." Please join us Sundays, 10 am to 2 pm. Or anytime. We're always 100% vegetarian and 100% delicious.

Café Voltaire
3231 North Clark Street Chicago, IL 60657 312-528-3136

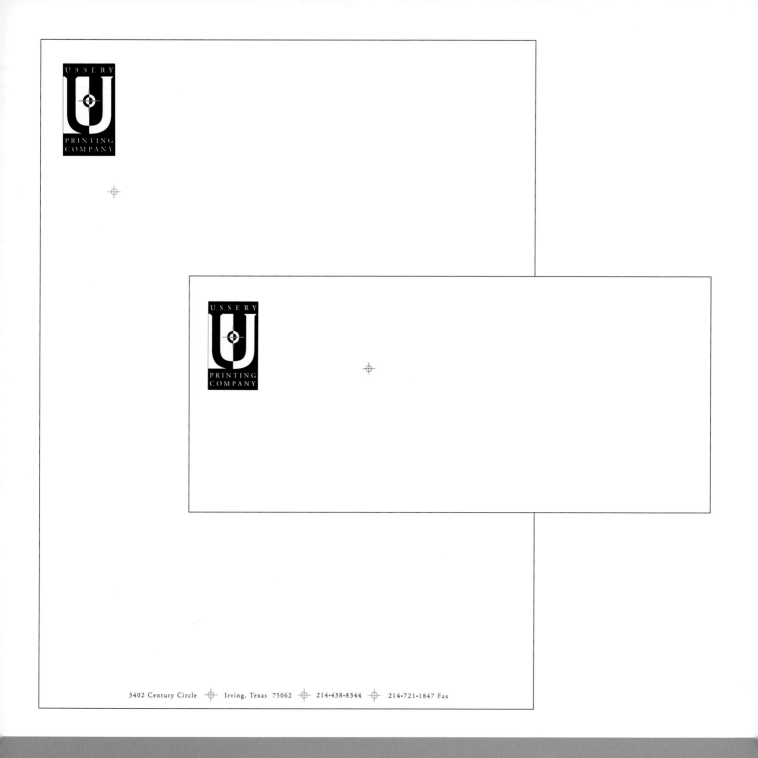

3402 Century Circle ✦ Irving, Texas 75062 ✦ 214•438•8344 ✦ 214•721•1847 Fax

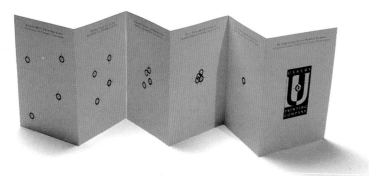

Ussery Printing Company

The black-and-white logo, in contrast to the more colorful logos of other printers, reinforces Ussery's commitment to small flat-color projects.

DESIGN FIRM: Tom Hair Marketing Design, Houston, Texas

ART DIRECTOR: Tom Hair

DESIGNERS: Bea Garcia, Tom Hair

BUDGET: Design (stationery): $2500; printing: in-house

PRINTING PROCESS: Flat PMS color; envelopes converted

123

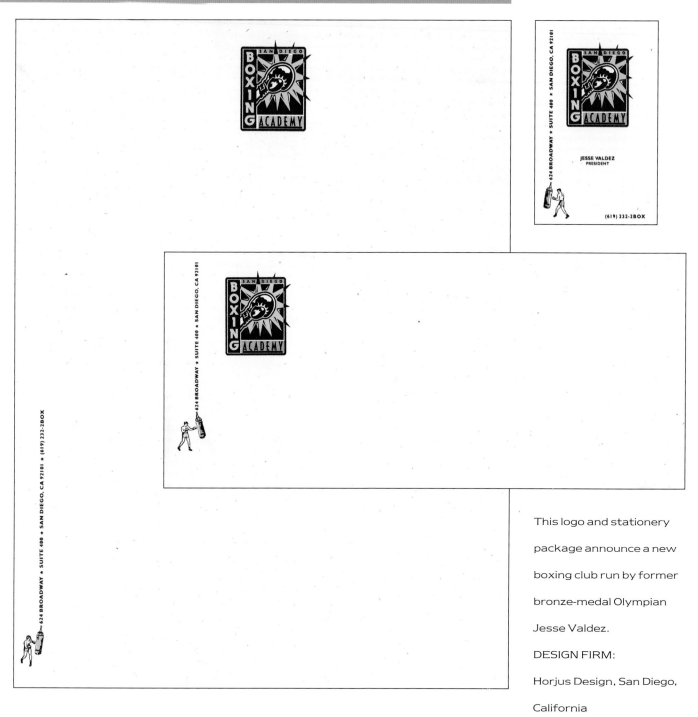

This logo and stationery
package announce a new
boxing club run by former
bronze-medal Olympian
Jesse Valdez.

DESIGN FIRM:

Horjus Design, San Diego,

California

DESIGNER/ILLUSTRATOR:

Peter Horjus

BUDGET: Design: $500;

printing: $725

PRINTING PROCESS:

4 PMS colors, 4-color offset

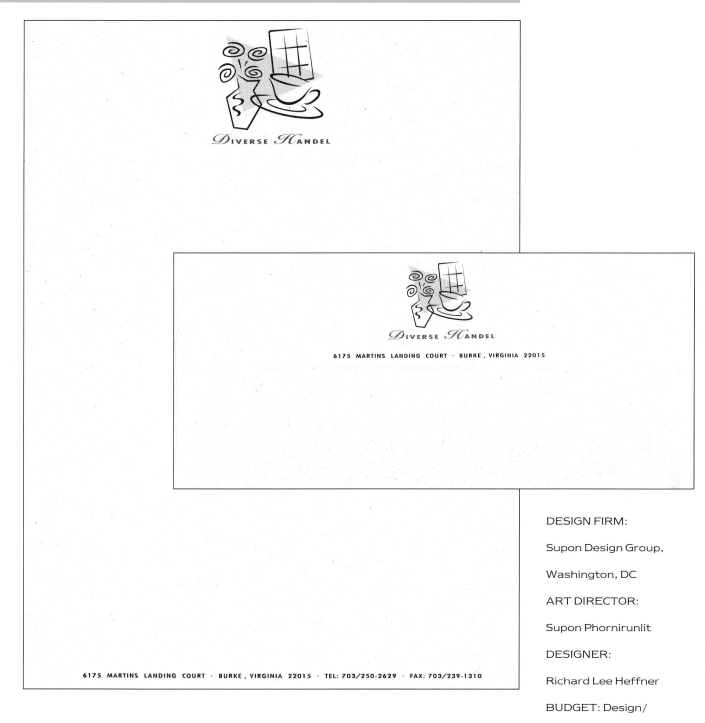

6175 MARTINS LANDING COURT · BURKE , VIRGINIA 22015 · TEL: 703/250-2629 · FAX: 703/239-1310

DESIGN FIRM:

Supon Design Group,

Washington, DC

ART DIRECTOR:

Supon Phornirunlit

DESIGNER:

Richard Lee Heffner

BUDGET: Design/

production: $1500;

printing: $2000

PRINTING PROCESS:

3-color

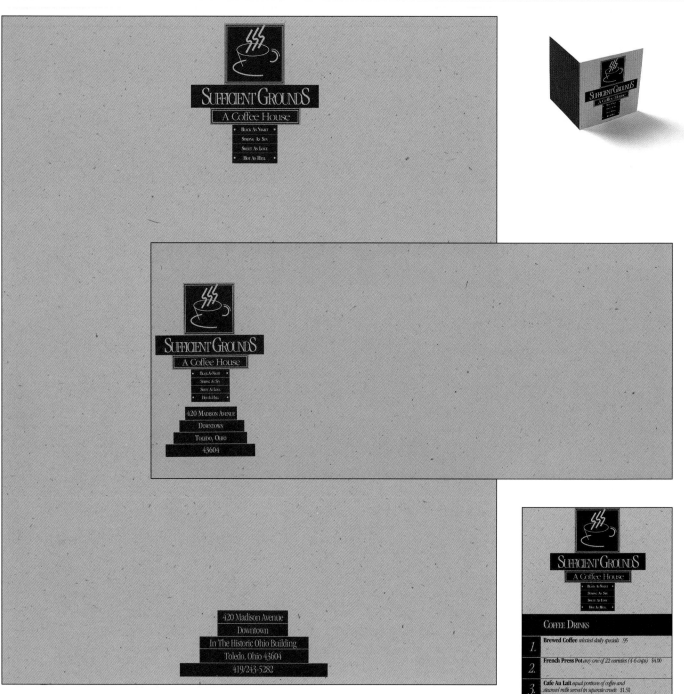

SUFFICIENT GROUNDS
A Coffee House

BLACK AS NIGHT
STRONG AS SIN
SWEET AS LOVE
HOT AS HELL

COFFEE DRINKS

1.	**Brewed Coffee** *selected daily specials* .95	
2.	**French Press Pot** *any one of 22 varieties (4-6 cups)* $4.00	
3.	**Cafe Au Lait** *equal portions of coffee and steamed milk served in separate cruets* $1.50	
4.	**Espresso** *finely ground coffee through which high pressure steam is forced* $1.00/$1.50	
5.	**Espresso Con Panna** *straight shot of espresso topped with whipped cream* $1.15/$1.65	
6.	**Cappuccino** *a serving of espresso with equal parts of steamed milk and rich, thick foam* $1.25/$1.75	
7.	**Macchiato** *a serving of espresso served with a spoonful of thick velvet foam* $1.20/$1.50	
8.	**Sufficient Cappuccino** *SG's delicious cappuccino steamed with your choice of Torani syrup* $1.55/$1.95	
9.	**Cafe Mocha** *a double espresso with steamed milk and chocolate syrup,topped with whipped cream and chocolate shavings- a chocolate lovers delight!!* sm. $1.90 lg. $2.10	
10.	**Caffe Latte** *an espresso with steamed milk topped with a small amount of foam* $1.60/$1.95	
11.	**Flavored Latte's** *a 12oz. latte served with a limitless variety of delicious flavor combinations* $2.00	

419/537-1988
This Also Functions ToGo

THE SUFFICIENT CLUB

If, as a member of the highly touted
"Sufficient Club", you purchase
any 10 coffee beverages,
Sufficient Grounds
will gratefully give you your next caffeine fix
Free of charge.
*Please be sure to have one of "The Efficient Sufficient People"
credit your club card and
enjoy every sip!*

GROUNDSTUFF

A MONTHLY PUBLICATION OF SUFFICIENT GROUNDS COFFEE HOUSE

WHAT ABOUT THOSE POTS

PUMP POTS

You may have noticed the vacuum air pots we use at Sufficient Grounds "Around the Corner" in which we serve our freshly brewed coffee. Brewed coffee is at its peak flavor the moment it has completed it's brewing cycle. The air pots keep coffee at this optimum temperature & flavor for up to two hours.

In days gone by, and in many restaurants even today, coffee is brewed into an open pot and placed on a burner that not only allows delicate oils with the essential flavor extracted from the bean to rapidly escape out the top, but imposes an increasingly bitter twist on the coffee's flavor due to continued heating.

The air pots keep coffee at this optimum temperature & flavor for up to two hours. They have an insulated glass lining that prevents evaporation and maintains near constant temperature. It means we are sure that the coffee we brew is the finest in quality, flavor, and aroma in town.

ENJOY!

Other tips to enjoy a quality cup of coffee at home.
- *Always start with cold water & with the right amount for the amount of coffee you are brewing.*
- *Make sure your coffee is ground to the right consistency Cone strapped –FINE Drip Filter – More Course*
- *If you are unsure of the mineral content of your water source, we recommend using bottled spring water or filtered water.*
- *Also since the finest beans in the world are available at Sufficient Grounds we highly recommend using our precious beans.*
- **Don't forget to get a Bean Club Card and get it punched often!**

FRENCH PRESS POTS

An exciting way to get a fresh, hot pot of coffee is the French Press method. At SG you can choose from any one of our 28 varieties of coffee and brew for yourself. The French Press method of brewing is thought by expert tasters to be the best method around. It leaves the essential oils and flavors of the beans in your coffee.

The French Press is as 1-2-3. You choose the coffee, we grind it coarsely and fill the pot with hot water. You let the coffee steep for about 4 minutes or until it gets to your desired color. Simply push the plunger to the bottom forcing all the grounds down leaving you with a rich, delicious pot of freshly brewed java.

The French Press Pots are great for home use, dinner parties, college students, and all coffee lovers. They are available in SG's retail section in different styles and sizes. Pick up a press pot at SG and start enjoying fabulous coffee the way it should be–just the way you like it.

BEANS TO YOU

$1.00 BEAN OFF

GOOD TO APRIL 30TH

PREFERRED BEAN

If, as a member of this highly touted "Preferred Bean" club, you purchase 9 luscious pounds of beans we will gratefully give you your 10th choice absolutely free. Please be sure to have one of "The Efficient Sufficient People" credit your club card and go forth to enjoy every sip!

A sophisticated look for a small local coffee house was created on a limited budget.
DESIGN FIRM: Weeks & Associates, Toledo, Ohio
DESIGNER: Dan Weeks
BUDGET: Design: $5500 (complete program); printing: $2200 for various items
PRINTING PROCESS: 1-color

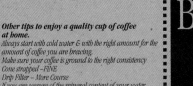

5893 OBERLIN DRIVE

SAN DIEGO CA 92121

800 876 7818 / 619 558 7800

WORKSTATIONS
ZZYZX
& PERIPHERALS

FAX 619 558 8283

E-MAIL:

ZZYZX!SALES@UCSD.EDU

WORKSTATIONS
ZZYZX
& PERIPHERALS

5893 OBERLIN DRIVE

SAN DIEGO CA 92121

A bold, strong identity is

projected by the logo for

this computer systems

reseller.

DESIGN FIRM:

Mires Design, Inc.,

San Diego, California

ART DIRECTOR: John Ball

PRINTING PROCESS:

3-color, offset

ZZYZX Workstation & Peripherals

WORKSTATIONS
ZZYZX
& PERIPHERALS

JOHN CAREY
PRESIDENT
5893 OBERLIN DRIVE
SAN DIEGO CA 92121
800 876 7818
619 558 7800
FAX 619 558 8283
E-MAIL:
ZZYZX!SALES@UCSD.EDU

DIGITAL SIGHT + SOUND

DIGITAL SIGHT + SOUND

14900 Landmark Boulevard
Suite 140
Dallas Texas 75240

14900 Landmark Boulevard
Suite 140
Dallas Texas 75240
214.702.1788
214.702.1789 *fax*

Digital Sight & Sound

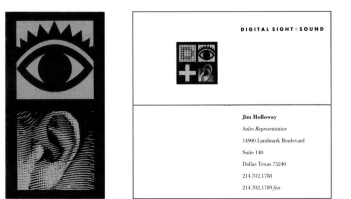

DIGITAL SIGHT + SOUND

Jim Holloway
Sales Representative
14900 Landmark Boulevard
Suite 140
Dallas Texas 75240
214.702.1788
214.702.1789 *fax*

A corporate identity package for a firm providing computers for illustrators and photographers.

DESIGN FIRM:

Gibbs Baronet, Dallas, Texas

ART DIRECTORS:

Steve Gibbs, Willie Baronet

DESIGNERS:

Kellye Kimball, Steve Gibbs

PRINTING PROCESS:

2-color, offset

A neurosurgeon opening a new practice wanted an atypical look for his stationery. The logo was enlarged to 4'-square and hung in his reception area.

DESIGN FIRM:

Dean Johnson Design, Inc.,

Indianapolis, Indiana

ART DIRECTOR/

DESIGNER/ILLUSTRATOR:

Mike Schwab

BUDGET: Design: $2000

PRINTING PROCESS:

4-color, offset

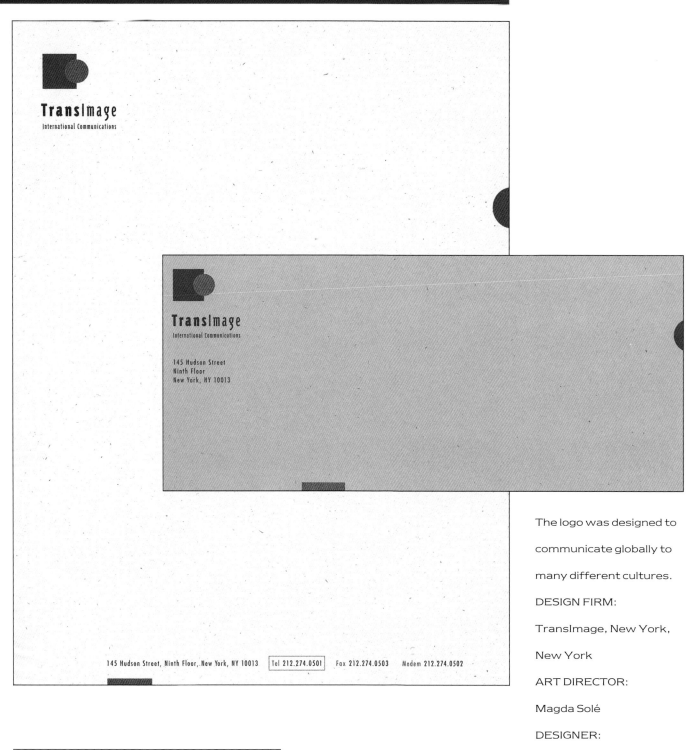

The logo was designed to communicate globally to many different cultures.

DESIGN FIRM:
TransImage, New York, New York

ART DIRECTOR:
Magda Solé

DESIGNER:
Lisa Bronson Mezoff

PRINTING PROCESS:
2 Pantone colors plus black, offset

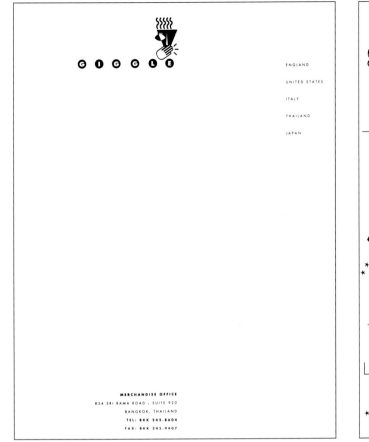

DESIGN FIRM:

Supon Design Group,

Washington, DC

ART DIRECTOR:

Supon Phornirunlit

DESIGNER:

Richard Lee Heffner

BUDGET: Design/

production: $2500;

printing: $800

PRINTING PROCESS:

Black only

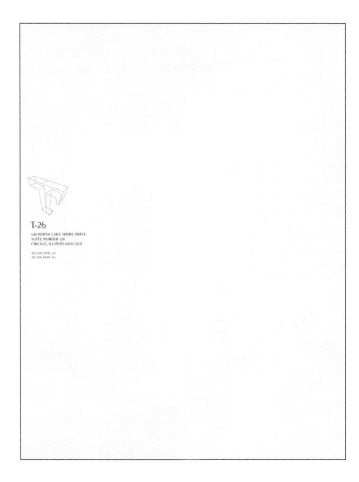

T-26

540 NORTH LAKE SHORE DRIVE
SUITE NUMBER 324
CHICAGO, ILLINOIS 60611.3431

312.670.TYPE tel
312.646.0640 fax

T-26 (Type Foundry)

DESIGN FIRM: Segura Inc.,

Chicago, Illinois

ART DIRECTOR/

DESIGNER: Carlos Segura

BUDGET: $3000 for 2000

letterheads

PRINTING PROCESS:

2-color (front), 1-color

(back)

This stationery package showcases every paper in the mill's industrial paper line (Dur-O-Tone). The spec box on each piece provides information on that particular paper.

DESIGN FIRM:

C.S. Anderson Design Company, Minneapolis, Minnesota

ART DIRECTOR/ ILLUSTRATOR:

Charles S. Anderson

DESIGNERS:

Charles S. Anderson, Todd Piper-Hauswirth

COPYWRITER:

Lisa Pemrick

BUDGET: $5000

PRINTING PROCESS:

Letterpress

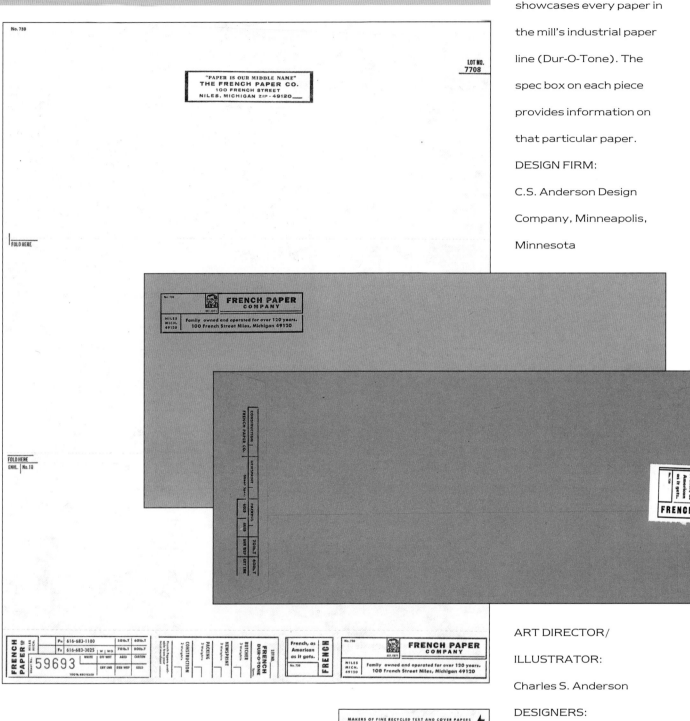

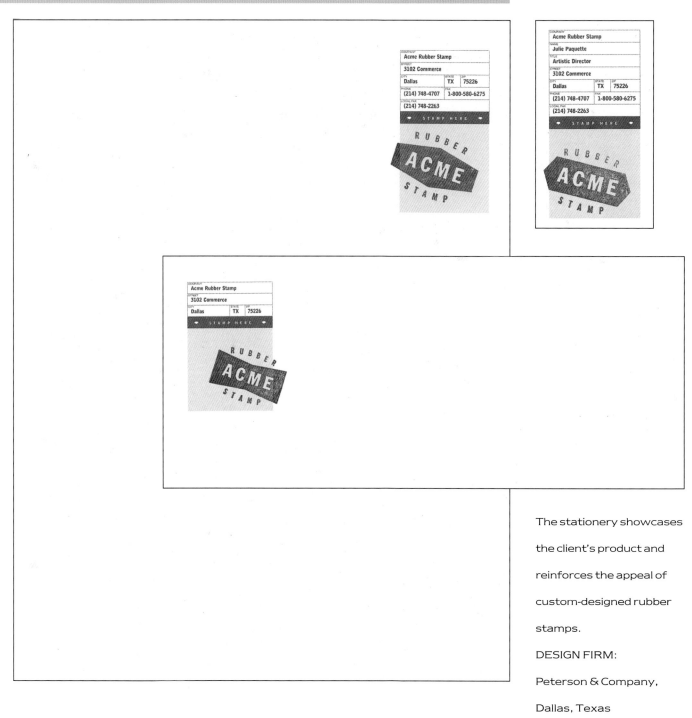

The stationery showcases the client's product and reinforces the appeal of custom-designed rubber stamps.

DESIGN FIRM:

Peterson & Company,

Dallas, Texas

ART DIRECTORS:

Bryan Peterson, Dave Eliason

BUDGET: Printing: $2800

PRINTING PROCESS:

2-color, rubber stamping

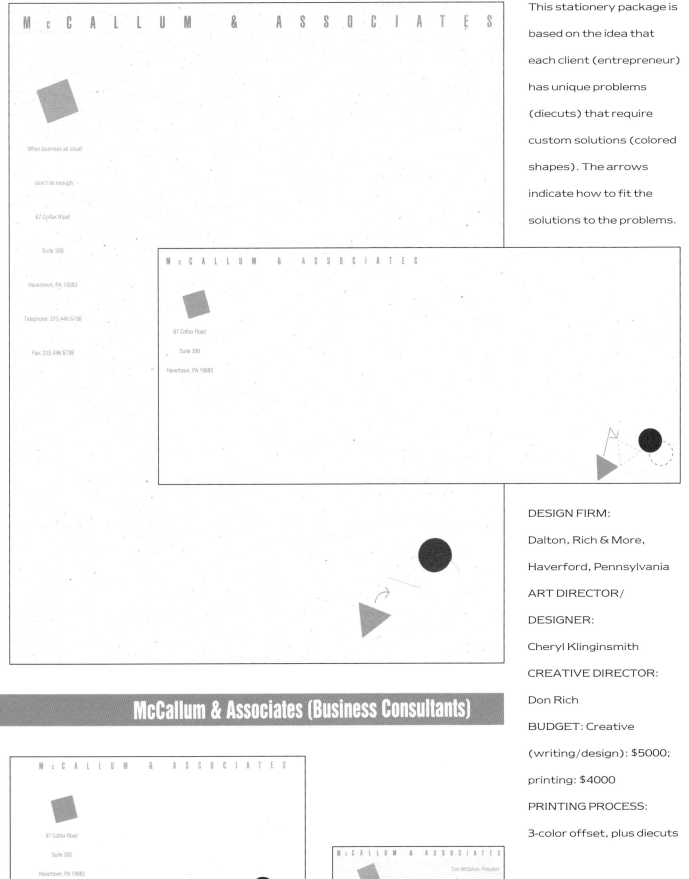

McCALLUM & ASSOCIATES

When business as usual

won't be enough.

67 Colfax Road

Suite 300

Havertown, PA 19083

Telephone: 215.446.6798

Fax: 215.446.6798

McCALLUM & ASSOCIATES

67 Colfax Road

Suite 300

Havertown, PA 19083

This stationery package is based on the idea that each client (entrepreneur) has unique problems (diecuts) that require custom solutions (colored shapes). The arrows indicate how to fit the solutions to the problems.

McCallum & Associates (Business Consultants)

McCALLUM & ASSOCIATES

67 Colfax Road

Suite 300

Havertown, PA 19083

McCALLUM & ASSOCIATES

Tom McCallum, President

67 Colfax Road, Suite 300

Havertown, PA 19083

Telephone: 215.446.6798

Fax: 215.446.6798

When business as usual won't be enough.

DESIGN FIRM:

Dalton, Rich & More,

Haverford, Pennsylvania

ART DIRECTOR/

DESIGNER:

Cheryl Klinginsmith

CREATIVE DIRECTOR:

Don Rich

BUDGET: Creative

(writing/design): $5000;

printing: $4000

PRINTING PROCESS:

3-color offset, plus diecuts

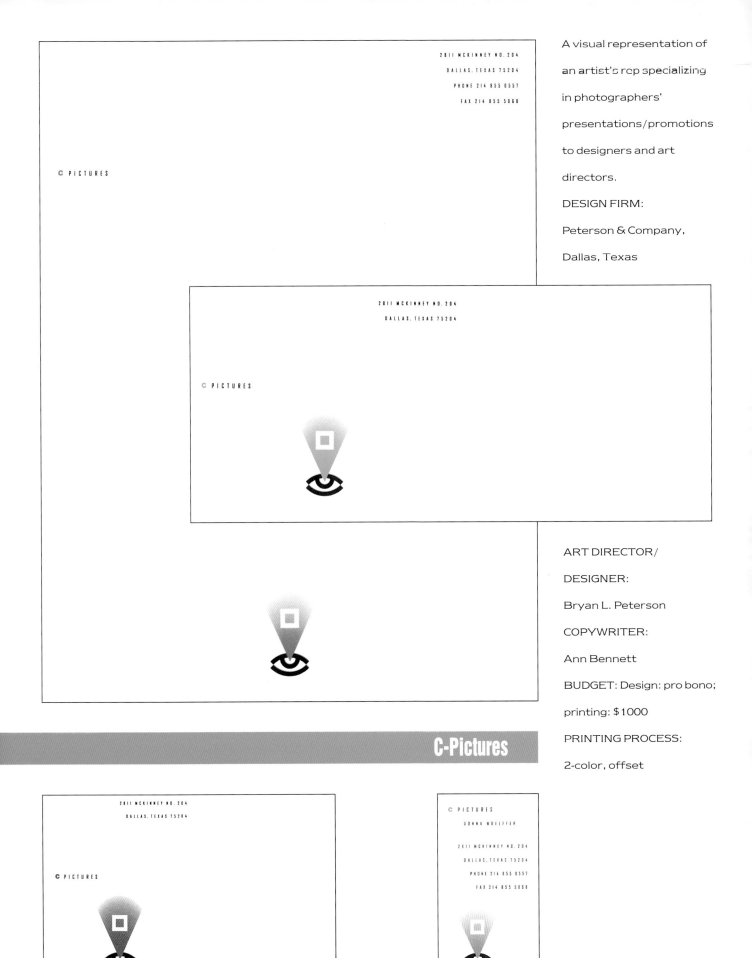

A visual representation of an artist's rep specializing in photographers' presentations/promotions to designers and art directors.

DESIGN FIRM:

Peterson & Company, Dallas, Texas

ART DIRECTOR/

DESIGNER:

Bryan L. Peterson

COPYWRITER:

Ann Bennett

BUDGET: Design: pro bono; printing: $1000

PRINTING PROCESS:

2-color, offset

C-Pictures

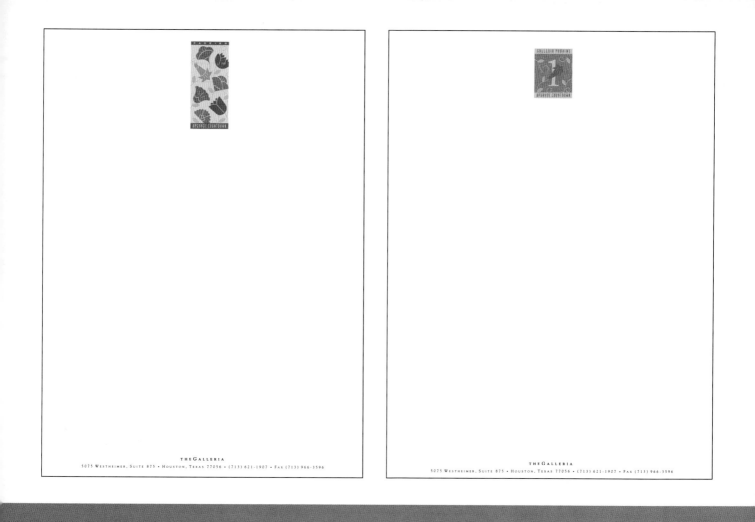

THEGALLERIA
5075 WESTHEIMER, SUITE 875 • HOUSTON, TEXAS 77056 • (713) 621-1907 • FAX (713) 966-3596

THEGALLERIA
5075 WESTHEIMER, SUITE 875 • HOUSTON, TEXAS 77056 • (713) 621-1907 • FAX (713) 966-3596

Stationery package designed for a public relations campaign promoting the upgrading of a shopping mall parking garage. The different symbols indicate the different garage levels.

DESIGN FIRM:

The Hill Group, Houston, Texas

ART DIRECTOR: Chris Hill

DESIGNERS: Jeff Davis, Tom Berno, Laura Menegaz

ILLUSTRATOR:

McRay Magleby

THEGALLERIA
5075 WESTHEIMER, SUITE 875 • HOUSTON, TEXAS 77056 • (713) 621-1907 • FAX (713) 966-3596

THE GALLERIA
5075 WESTHEIMER, SUITE 875 • HOUSTON, TEXAS 77056 • (713) 621-1907 • FAX (713) 966-3596

THE GALLERIA
5075 WESTHEIMER, SUITE 875 • HOUSTON, TEXAS 77056 • (713) 621-1907 • FAX (713) 966-3596

The Galleria (Shopping Mall)

THE GALLERIA

THE GALLERIA

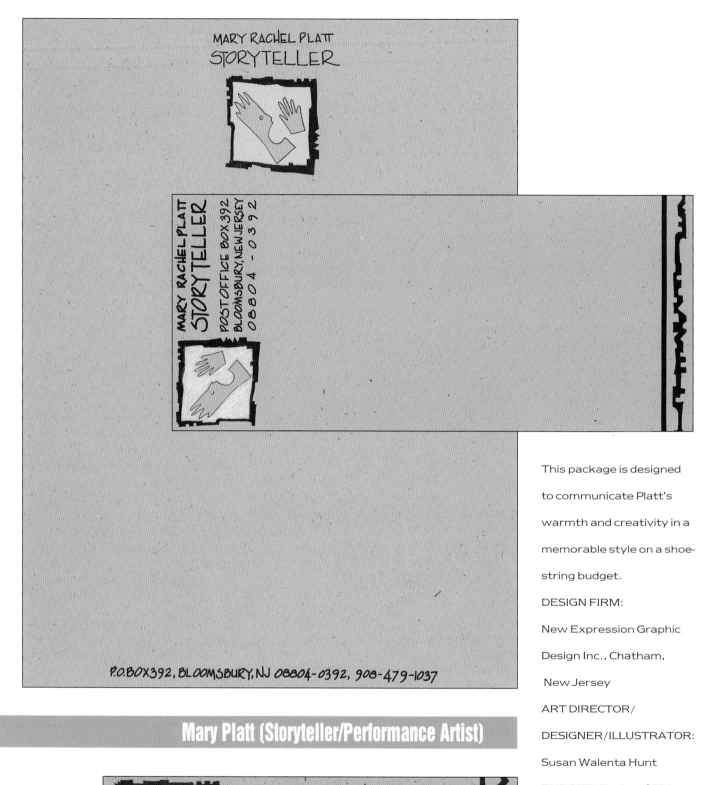

This package is designed to communicate Platt's warmth and creativity in a memorable style on a shoe-string budget.

DESIGN FIRM:

New Expression Graphic Design Inc., Chatham, New Jersey

ART DIRECTOR/ DESIGNER/ILLUSTRATOR: Susan Walenta Hunt

BUDGET: Design: $500 (initial budget)

PRINTING PROCESS: 1- and 2-color, offset

Mary Platt (Storyteller/Performance Artist)

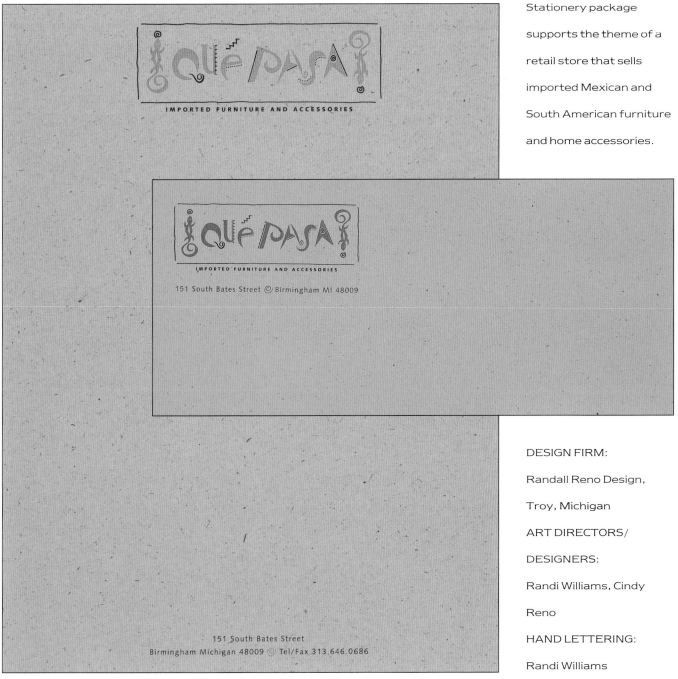

Stationery package supports the theme of a retail store that sells imported Mexican and South American furniture and home accessories.

DESIGN FIRM:

Randall Reno Design,

Troy, Michigan

ART DIRECTORS/

DESIGNERS:

Randi Williams, Cindy

Reno

HAND LETTERING:

Randi Williams

BUDGET: Design: $250;

printing: $600

PRINTING PROCESS:

2 PMS colors on each

piece (except packaging)

Que Pasa Furniture & Accessories

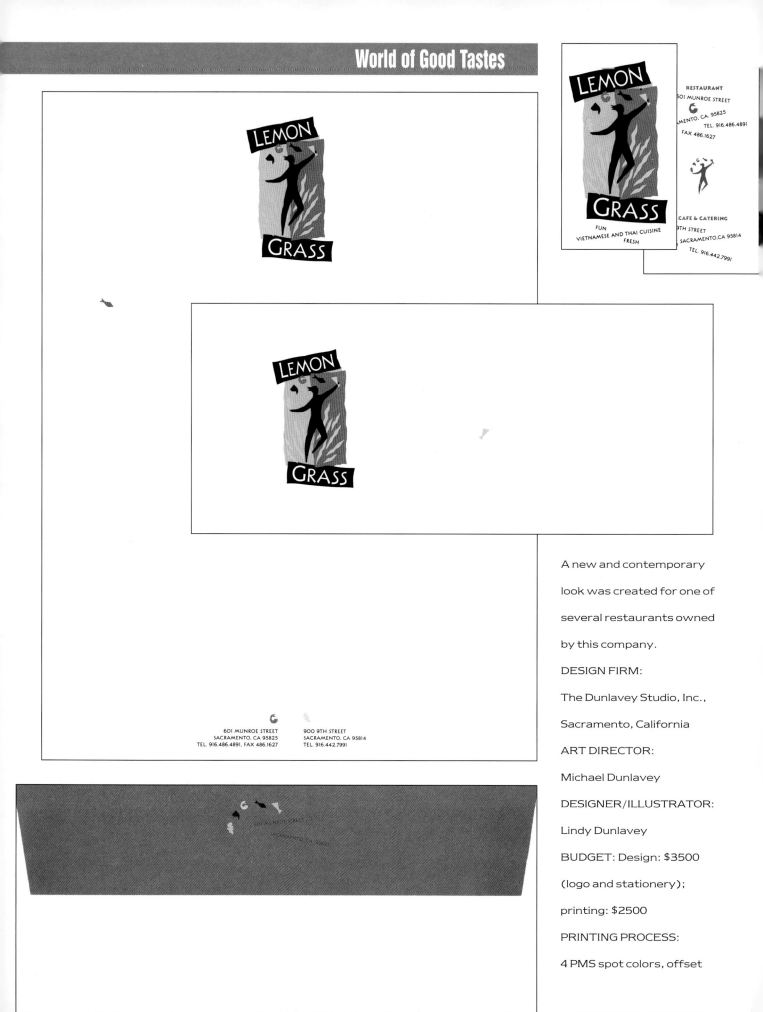

A new and contemporary
look was created for one of
several restaurants owned
by this company.

DESIGN FIRM:

The Dunlavey Studio, Inc.,

Sacramento, California

ART DIRECTOR:

Michael Dunlavey

DESIGNER/ILLUSTRATOR:

Lindy Dunlavey

BUDGET: Design: $3500

(logo and stationery);

printing: $2500

PRINTING PROCESS:

4 PMS spot colors, offset

601 MUNROE STREET
SACRAMENTO, CA 95825
TEL. 916.486.4891, FAX 486.1627

900 9TH STREET
SACRAMENTO, CA 95814
TEL. 916.442.7991

Julie Swanson

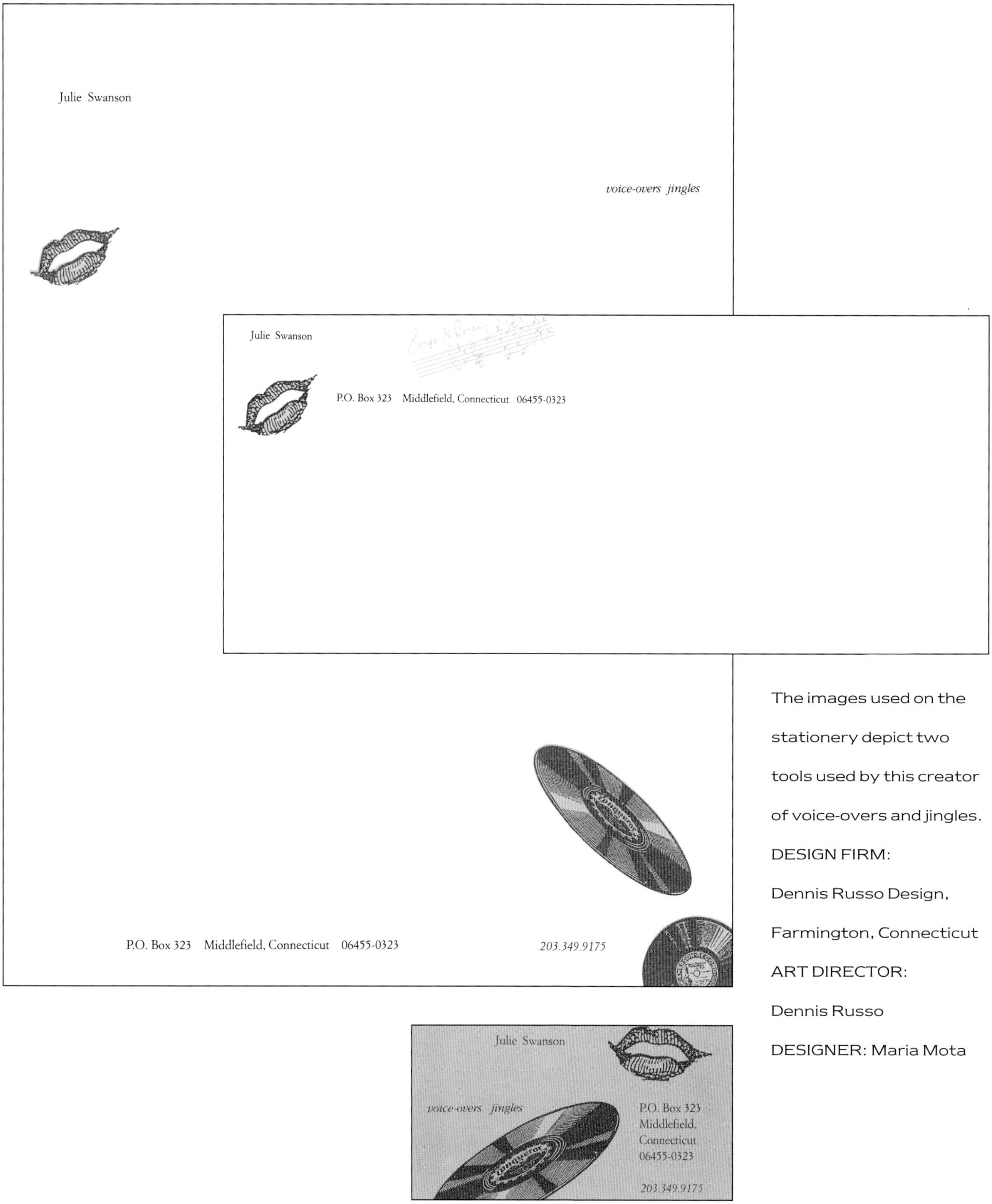

voice-overs jingles

Julie Swanson

P.O. Box 323   Middlefield, Connecticut   06455-0323

P.O. Box 323   Middlefield, Connecticut   06455-0323

203.349.9175

Julie Swanson

voice-overs jingles

P.O. Box 323
Middlefield,
Connecticut
06455-0323

203.349.9175

The images used on the
stationery depict two
tools used by this creator
of voice-overs and jingles.
DESIGN FIRM:
Dennis Russo Design,
Farmington, Connecticut
ART DIRECTOR:
Dennis Russo
DESIGNER: Maria Mota

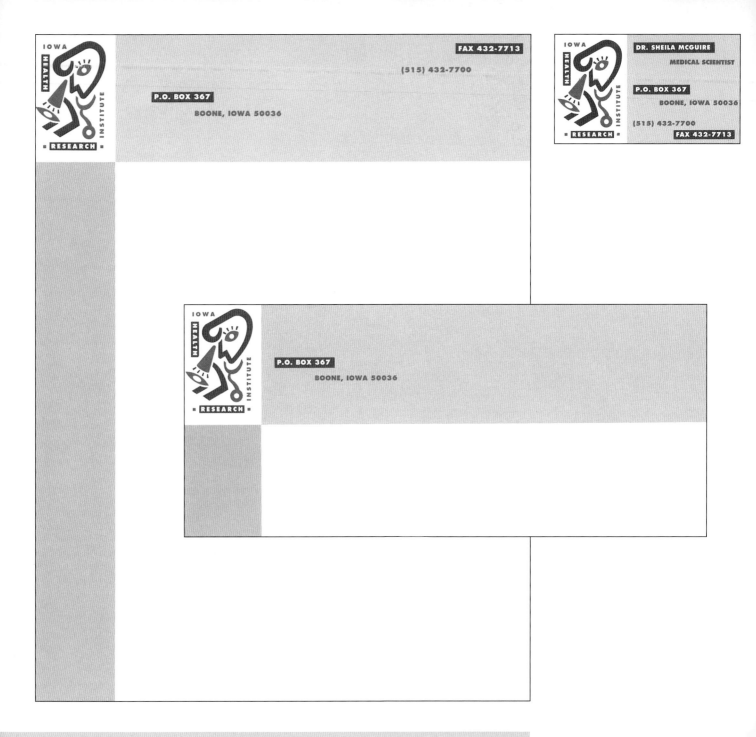

IOWA HEALTH RESEARCH INSTITUTE (logo)

FAX 432-7713

(515) 432-7700

P.O. BOX 367
BOONE, IOWA 50036

DR. SHEILA MCGUIRE
MEDICAL SCIENTIST

P.O. BOX 367
BOONE, IOWA 50036

(515) 432-7700
FAX 432-7713

P.O. BOX 367
BOONE, IOWA 50036

Iowa Health Research Institute

This health research facility sought to present a different image of a field traditionally thought of as ultra-conservative and a bit stodgy. They achieved this goal with a graphic logo and interesting use of color and, at the same time, positioned themselves as competent yet innovative in their approach to health issues.

DESIGN FIRM:

Sayles Graphic Design, Des Moines, Iowa

DESIGNER: John Sayles

PRINTING PROCESS:

2 colors, offset

144

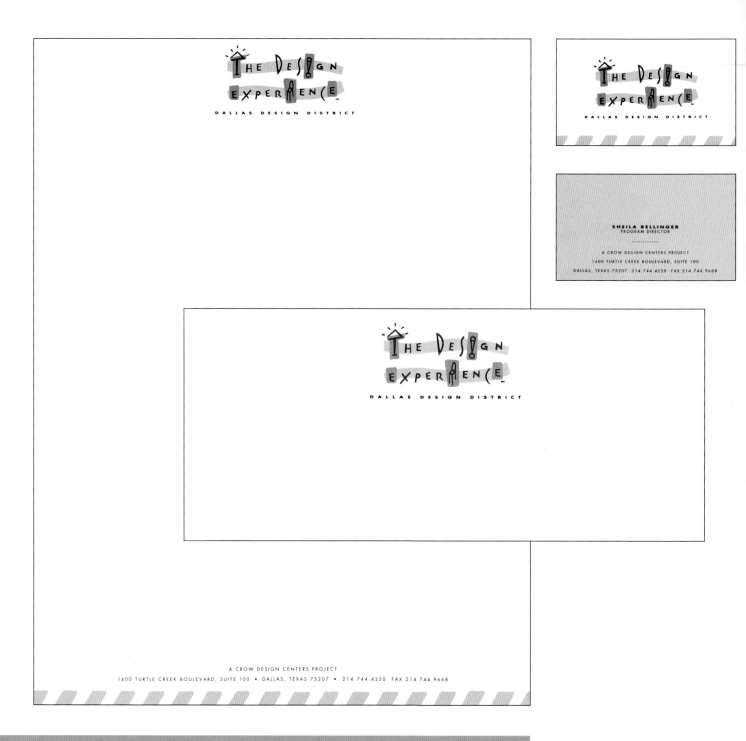

The Design Experience (Interior Design)

Package promotes a firm that is a new part of The Design District, which is open to the public and where people go to find designers, architects, fabrics, furniture, etc.

DESIGN FIRM:

Jon Flaming Design, Dallas, Texas

ART DIRECTORS:

Jon Flaming, Jim Hradecky

DESIGNER/ILLUSTRATOR:

Jon Flaming

BUDGET: Design: $5000; printing: $7500

PRINTING PROCESS:

Offset, 5-color

145

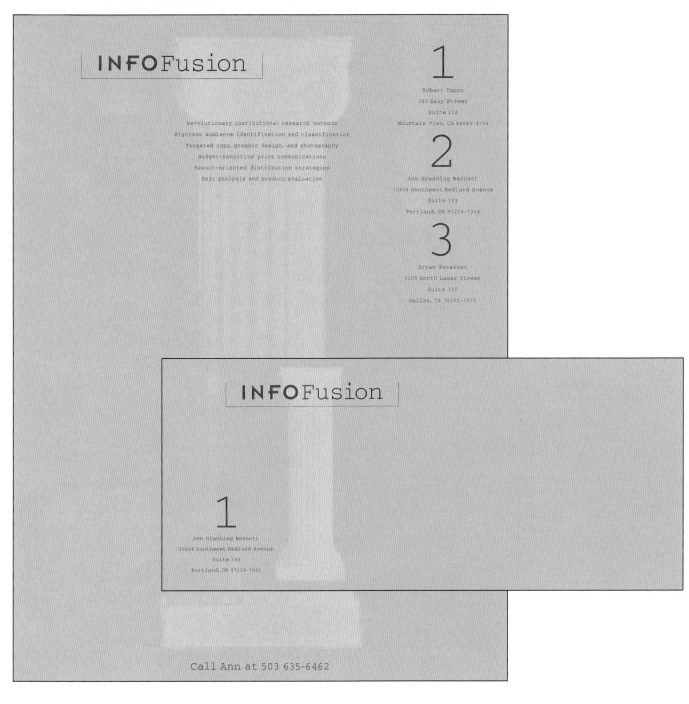

The stationery was designed as an information piece to communicate INFOFusion's capabilities to clients and potential clients seeking assistance with institutional research,

marketing, writing and design.

DESIGN FIRM: Peterson & Company, Dallas, Texas

ART DIRECTOR/ DESIGNER: Bryan Peterson

BUDGET: Design: pro bono; printing: $2500

PRINTING PROCESS: 2 PMS colors + white, offset

COPY.

ONOMATOPOEIA.

PERSONIFICATION.

OXYMORON.

ALLITERATION.

· · · · · · · ·

I THINK

ABOUT ALL THIS

STUFF.

· · · · · · · ·

SO YOU DON'T

HAVE TO.

ELLEN McBRIDE
COPYWRITER

· · · · · · · ·

4810

HAYMARKET

DRIVE.

VIRGINIA BEACH

VIRGINIA

23462

804 | 467 | 7067

COMMA.

DASH.

SEMICOLON.

QUESTION MARK.

EXCLAMATION POINT.

ELLEN McBRIDE
COPYWRITER

PERIOD.

· · · · · · · ·

4810
HAYMARKET DRIVE
VIRGINIA BEACH
VIRGINIA 23462

THERE
ARE 800,000
WORDS
IN THE
ENGLISH
LANGUAGE.
· · · · · · · ·
ONLY
A HANDFUL
ARE RIGHT
AT ANY GIVEN
TIME.

AND
I KNOW
JUST
WHAT
THEY
ARE.

ELLEN McBRIDE
COPYWRITER
· · · · · · · ·
4810
HAYMARKET
DRIVE
VIRGINIA BEACH
VIRGINIA
23462
804 | 467 | 7067

The stationery speaks for itself, using the techniques and tools of writing to promote McBride's capabilities to advertising agencies, clients and freelance art directors.

DESIGN FIRM:
Morris Design, Norfolk, Virginia
ART DIRECTOR/
DESIGNER: Bart Morris
COPYWRITER:
Ellen McBride

BUDGET: Design: in-trade for dinner; printing: $750
PRINTING PROCESS:
2-color, offset at
Sir Speedy Printing
PAPER: Graphika
(different colors)

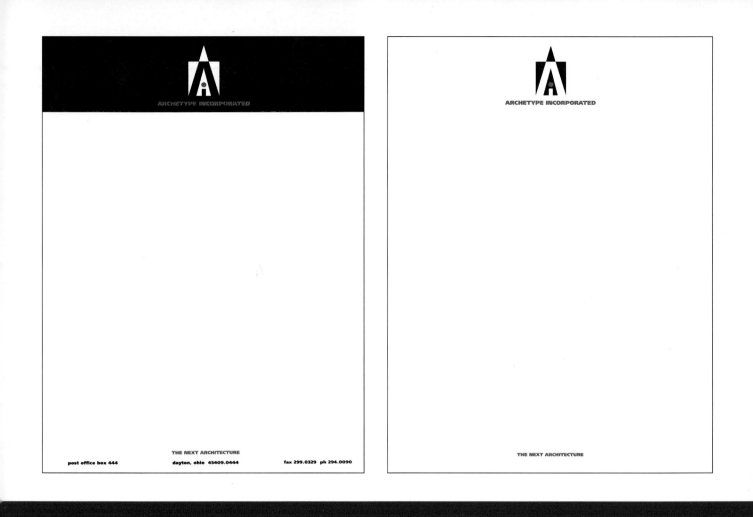

THE NEXT ARCHITECTURE

post office box 444 dayton, ohio 45409.0444 fax 299.0329 ph 294.0090

THE NEXT ARCHITECTURE

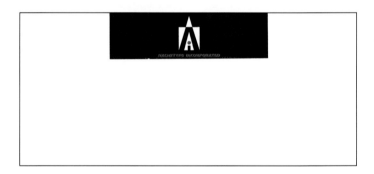

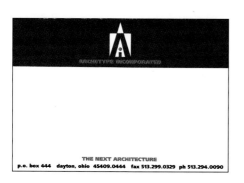

THE NEXT ARCHITECTURE

post office box 444   dayton, ohio 45409.0444   fax 299.0329 ph 294.0090

Stationery and corporate identity package for a new group of architects specializing in commercial space who wanted something clean and powerful that reflected their love of the Bauhaus. French's Butcher White paper was chosen because it adds a modeled look to solid ink coverage, giving an added, elegant dimension to a 2-color piece.

DESIGN FIRM:
Real Art Design Group, Inc., Dayton, Ohio

ART DIRECTOR/ DESIGNER: Chris Wire

BUDGET: Design: in trade for architectural services; printing: $2000

PRINTING PROCESS: 2-color (PMS 185 and black), offset (Itek 3985)

Archetype, Inc. (Architecture)

THE NEXT ARCHITECTURE

p.o. box 444   dayton, ohio   45409.0444   fax 513.299.0329   ph 513.294.0090

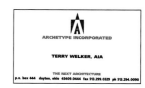

ARCHETYPE INCORPORATED

TERRY WELKER, AIA

THE NEXT ARCHITECTURE

p.o. box 444   dayton, ohio   45409.0444   fax 513.299.0329   ph 513.294.0090

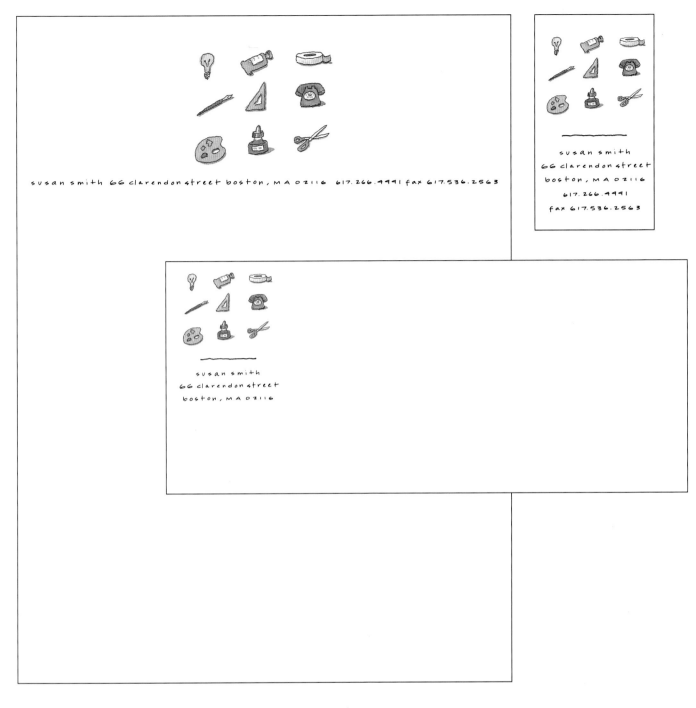

Susan Smith (Design/Illustration)

DESIGN FIRM:

Beth Carlisle Design,

Needham, Massachusetts

ART DIRECTOR/

DESIGNER: Beth Carlisle

ILLUSTRATOR:

Susan Smith

BUDGET: $1500

PRINTING PROCESS:

4-color

P.O. Box 7353

Cumberland, RI 02864

401-333-1013

P.O. Box 7353, Cumberland, RI 02864

Gerry Plante (Custom Painting/Paperhanging)

To emphasize the colorful nature of Plante's custom interior and paperhanging business, a different second color is used on each element of the stationery package. His trademark—signing his work under the last sheet of wallpaper—is used as a statement of quality.

DESIGN FIRM: Adkins-Balchunas Design, Pawtucket, Rhode Island

ART DIRECTOR/ DESIGNER: Jerry Balchunas

ILLUSTRATOR: Carl Bolton

BUDGET: Design: $1200; printing: $650

PRINTING PROCESS: Offset

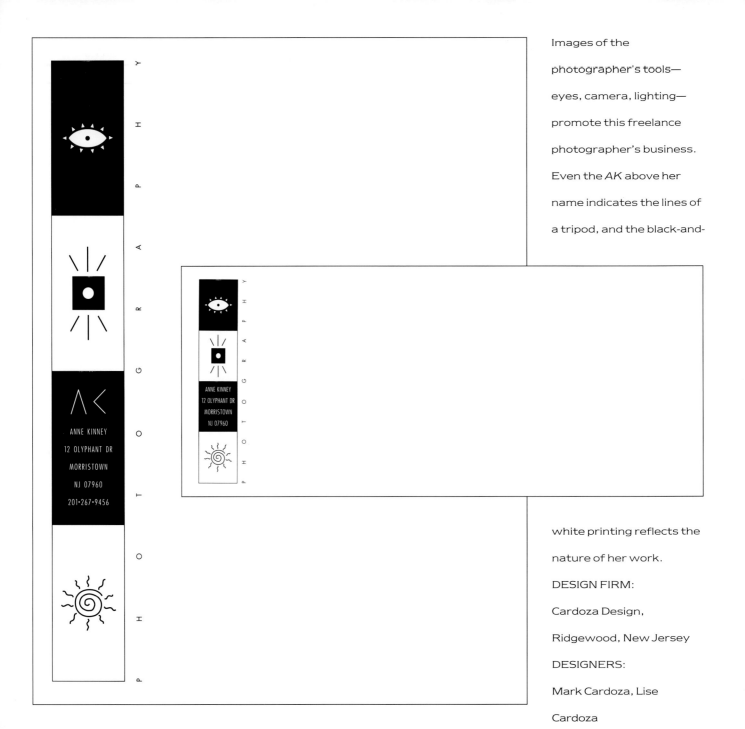

Images of the photographer's tools—eyes, camera, lighting—promote this freelance photographer's business. Even the *AK* above her name indicates the lines of a tripod, and the black-and-white printing reflects the nature of her work.

DESIGN FIRM:
Cardoza Design, Ridgewood, New Jersey

DESIGNERS:
Mark Cardoza, Lise Cardoza

BUDGET: Design: $500; printing: $350

PRINTING PROCESS:
Offset lithography

Anne Kinney (Photographer)

PHOTTOGRAPHY

DESIGN FIRM:

Dennard Creative, Inc.,

Dallas, Texas

ART DIRECTOR:

Bob Dennard

DESIGNER: Chris Wood

PRINTING PROCESS:

2-color, offset

PHOTTOGRAPHY

JEFF OTT PHOTOGRAPHY
2328 FARRINGTON, DALLAS, TEXAS 75207

JEFF OTT PHOTOGRAPHY
2328 FARRINGTON DALLAS, TEXAS 75207
PHONE 214-638-0602, FAX 638-0316

Jeff Ott Photography

PHOTTOGRAPHY

JEFF OTT PHOTOGRAPHY
2328 FARRINGTON DALLAS, TEXAS 75207
PHONE 214-638-0602, FAX 638-0316

PHOTTOGRAPHY

JEFF OTT

JEFF OTT PHOTOGRAPHY
2328 FARRINGTON DALLAS, TEXAS 75207
PHONE 214-638-0602, FAX 638-0316

153

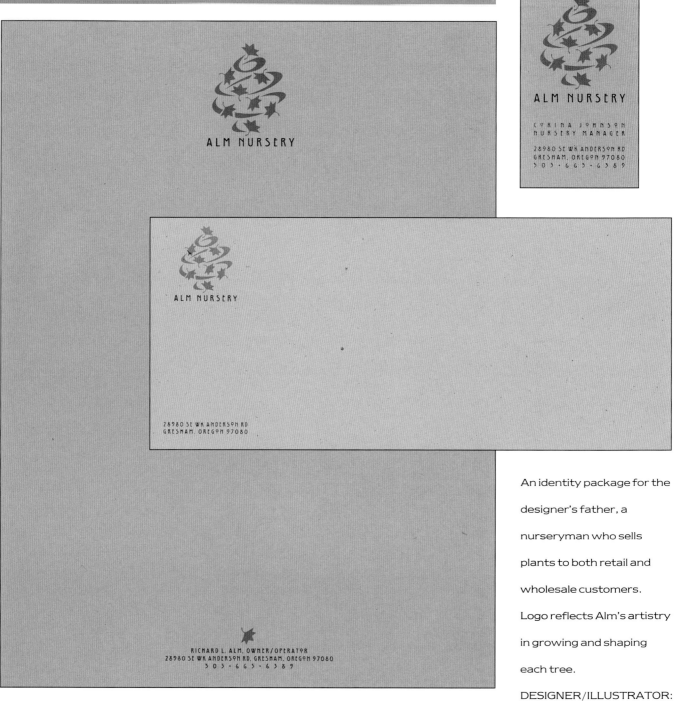

ALM NURSERY

CORINA JOHNSON
NURSERY MANAGER
28980 SE WK ANDERSON RD
GRESHAM, OREGON 97080
303·665·6389

ALM NURSERY

ALM NURSERY

28980 SE WK ANDERSON RD
GRESHAM, OREGON 97080

RICHARD L. ALM, OWNER/OPERATOR
28980 SE WK ANDERSON RD, GRESHAM, OREGON 97080
303·665·6389

An identity package for the designer's father, a nurseryman who sells plants to both retail and wholesale customers. Logo reflects Alm's artistry in growing and shaping each tree.

DESIGNER/ILLUSTRATOR: Brian Alm, Seattle, Washington

BUDGET: $2000

PRINTING PROCESS: 2-color (2 passes through a 1-color press)

This stationery package establishes a visual identity for a new Off Off Broadway theater; conveys a professional image to patrons, press, and potential funders; and expresses the philosophy of a theater dedicated to a co-operative environment— a place (home) where artists can work and grow.

DESIGN FIRM:
Stacie Cowan Gray Design, New York, New York

ART DIRECTOR/
DESIGNER:
Stacie Cowan Gray

BUDGET: Design: pro bono; printing: $1000

PRINTING PROCESS:
2-color, silkscreen

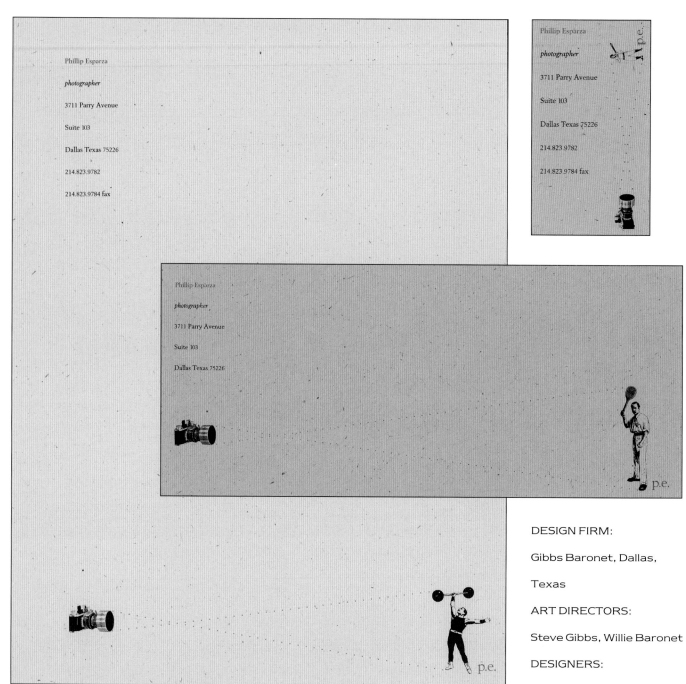

Phillip Esparza

photographer

3711 Parry Avenue

Suite 103

Dallas Texas 75226

214.823.9782

214.823.9784 fax

DESIGN FIRM:

Gibbs Baronet, Dallas,

Texas

ART DIRECTORS:

Steve Gibbs, Willie Baronet

DESIGNERS:

Kellye Kimball, Steve Gibbs

PRINTING PROCESS:

2-color, offset

Phillip Esparza (Photographer)

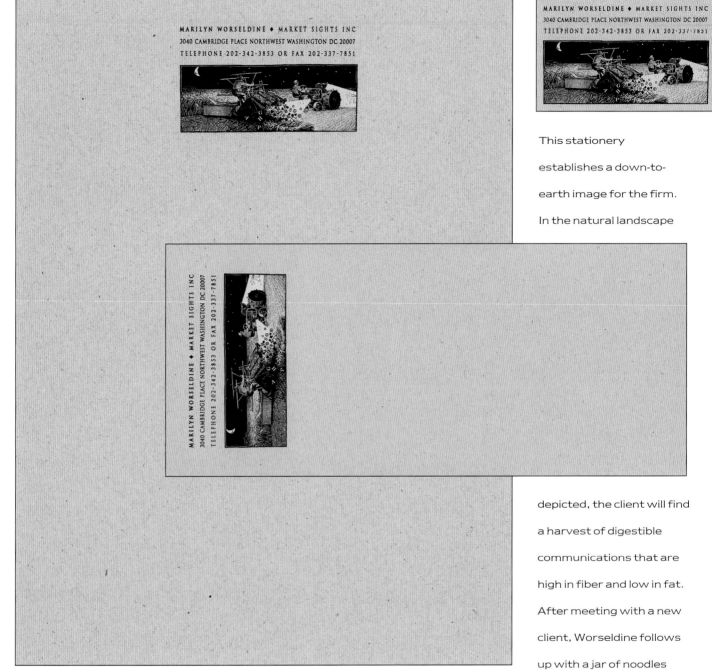

This stationery establishes a down-to-earth image for the firm. In the natural landscape depicted, the client will find a harvest of digestible communications that are high in fiber and low in fat. After meeting with a new client, Worseldine follows up with a jar of noodles and a note of thanks.

DESIGN FIRM:
Market Sights, Inc.,
Washington, DC
DESIGNER:
Marilyn Worseldine
BUDGET: $350 for 500
of each item
PRINTING PROCESS:
2-color, offset

Market Sights, Inc. (Graphic Design)

This multi-purpose stationery is used for correspondence with suppliers and for press releases announcing lectures and book signings held at the store and price listings distributed at book fairs and the like.

DESIGN FIRM:

Never Boring Design,

Modesto, California

ART DIRECTOR:

David Boring

DESIGNER/ILLUSTRATOR:

Virgil Mayol

BUDGET: Design (logo and stationery): $1500; printing: $600

PRINTING PROCESS:

3-color (2PMS plus black)

PINZETTE
GlassWorks

Michael Sosin
2547 Eighth Street
Berkeley, California
94710
510.649.8952

PINZETTE
GlassWorks

PINZETTE
GlassWorks

2547 Eighth Street
Berkeley, California
94710

2547 Eighth Street
Berkeley, California
94710
510.649.8952

Michael Sosin, a dentist,

needed an identity for

his other business:

glassblowing. The result

is this charming stationery

package.

DESIGN FIRM:

Kinde Nebeker Design,

Salt Lake City, Utah

ART DIRECTOR/

DESIGNER/ILLUSTRATOR:

Kinde Nebeker

BUDGET: Design: $350;

printing: $600

PRINTING PROCESS:

3 PMS colors

An Information Center for Young Children with Special Needs

334 N. Topeka, Suite 100

Wichita, Kansas

ZIP CODE 67202

PH. 316.267.3535

An Information Center for Young Children with Special Needs

334 N. Topeka, Suite 100 Wichita, Ks.
ZIP CODE 67202

Suzanne Chapel-Miller, LBSW
SOCIAL SERVICE COORDINATOR

334 N. Topeka, Suite 100
Wichita, Ks. 67202
PH. 316 . 267 . 3535

AN INFORMATION CENTER FOR YOUNG CHILDREN WITH SPECIAL NEEDS

Connecting Point

This image update for an information referral service for children with special needs has a friendly, child-like quality, while also denoting a source of support and caring. The unusual shape and size of the business card has had an unexpected result at local events—children can't seem to keep their hands off the cards and often are the first to give them to their parents.

DESIGN FIRM:
Love Packaging Group, Wichita, Kansas

ART DIRECTOR/
DESIGNER/ILLUSTRATOR:
Brian Miller

BUDGET: Design (logo and stationery package): $300; printing: $600

PRINTING PROCESS:
3-color, offset

Identity program launching

a new restaurant that

specializes in delivery.

DESIGN FIRM:

Mc Squared, Los Angeles,

California

ART DIRECTOR:

Ron McMillan

DESIGNER:

Stacey McClannan

PRINTING PROCESS:

4-color

Sunset Place

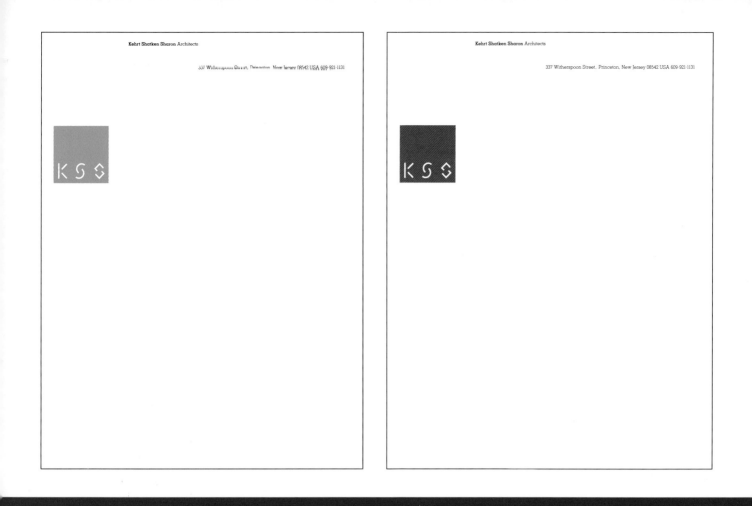

Kehrt Shatken Sharon Architects

337 Witherspoon Street, Princeton, New Jersey 08542 USA 609-921-1131

Kehrt Shatken Sharon Architects

337 Witherspoon Street, Princeton, New Jersey 08542 USA 609-921-1131

337 Witherspoon Street, Princeton, New Jersey 08542 USA

Kehrt Shatken Sharon Architects

337 Witherspoon Street, Princeton, New Jersey 08542 USA

Kehrt Shatken Sharon Architects

Kehrt Shatken Sharon Architects

Allan W Kehrt AIA

337 Witherspoon Street
Princeton, New Jersey 08542
609-921-1131

Kehrt Shatken Sharon Architects

Rafael H Sharon AIA

337 Witherspoon Street
Princeton, New Jersey 08542
609-921-1131

Kehrt Shatken Sharon Architects

337 Witherspoon Street, Princeton, New Jersey 08542 USA 609·921·1131

K S S

337 Witherspoon Street, Princeton, New Jersey 08542 USA

Kehrt Shatken Sharon Architects

K S S

337 Witherspoon Street, Princeton, New Jersey 08542 USA

Kehrt Shatken Sharon Architects

K S S

337 Witherspoon Street, Princeton, New Jersey 08542 USA

Kehrt Shatken Sharon Architects

K S S

Kehrt Shatken Sharon (Architects)

337 Witherspoon Street, Princeton, New Jersey 08542 USA

Kehrt Shatken Sharon Architects

K S S

Kehrt Shatken Sharon Architects

Michael C Shatken AIA

337 Witherspoon Street
Princeton, New Jersey 08542
609·921·1131

K S S

DESIGN FIRM:

Cook and Shanosky

Associates, Inc.,

Newton, Pennsylvania

ART DIRECTORS:

Roger Cook, Don Shanosky

DESIGNER:

Douglas Baszczuk

PRINTING PROCESS:

4 match colors, offset

163

Rapid Design Services
Rapid Typographers
Rapid Lasergraphics

R A P I D

Production Management

Design

Layout

Comps

Heroes

Line Art

Illustration

Computer Graphics

Type Specification

Typography

Photostats

Modifications

Distortions

Color Rubdowns

Color Drawdowns

Mechanicals

Disk Conversions

Scanning

Digital Color Separation

Canon Color Copies

Canon Digital Proofs

Dupont 4Cast Proofs

Iris Proofs

Linotronic Output

Matchprints

Koll Business Park
574 Weddell Drive #6
Sunnyvale CA 94089
Facsimile 408 747 0263
Telephone 408 747 1466

R A P I D

A new identity signaled RAPID's transformation from a traditional typesetting shop into a full-service prepress company offering a broad range of services. The redesign promotes the shop's use of advanced technology and its color separation capabilities.

RAPID (Electronic Prepress and Service Bureau)

Bent Kjolby
President

R A P I D

Rapid Design Services
Rapid Typographers
Rapid Lasergraphics

One Jackson Place
633 Battery Street
San Francisco CA 94111
Facsimile 415 982 5820
Telephone 415 982 6071

R A P I D

Digital Pre-press   One Jackson Place   Facsimile 415 989 5820
Typography   633 Battery Street   Telephone 415 982 6071
Design Services   San Francisco CA 94111

DESIGN FIRM:

Landkamer Design,

San Francisco, California

DESIGNER:

Mark Landkamer

ILLUSTRATORS:

Mark Landkamer,

Jym Warhol

BUDGET: Design/final art:

$15,000

PRINTING PROCESS:

4 match colors, offset

lithography

A clean, contemporary identity promoted the 1994 AspenWorld conference to a worldwide audience and unified support material for the event.

DESIGN FIRM:
Stewart Monderer Design, Inc., Boston, Massachusetts

ART DIRECTOR:
Stewart Monderer
DESIGNER:
Felipe Del Corral
PRINTING PROCESS:
4-color, offset

Aspen Technology, Inc. (Process Modeling Software)

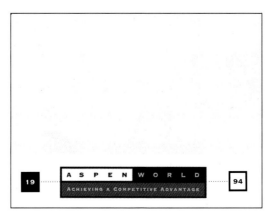

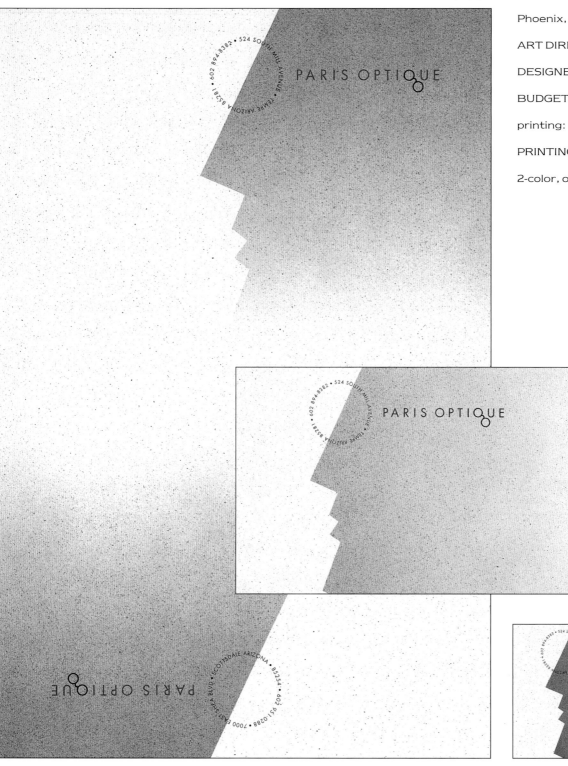

DESIGN FIRM:

Smit Ghormley Lofgreen,

Phoenix, Arizona

ART DIRECTOR/

DESIGNER: Art Lofgreen

BUDGET: Design: $5000;

printing: $3000

PRINTING PROCESS:

2-color, offset

ATLANTA
VISION
IN
DESIGN

1201
WEST
PEACHTREE
STREET
SUITE 3630
ATLANTA, GA
30309
404 873 AVID

This consortium of Atlanta-based designers was formed to communicate the vision and sophistication of the local design community to the Atlanta Committee for the Olympic Games and national media audiences. It avidly espoused the involvement of southern themes and southern design professionals in the look of the 1996 Atlanta Games.

DESIGN FIRM:
Wages Design, Atlanta, Georgia
ART DIRECTOR/
DESIGNER: Ted Fabella
ILLUSTRATOR:
Kevin Kemmerly
COPYWRITER:
Matthew Porter
PRINTING PROCESS:
3-color, offset

ATLANTA
VISION
IN
DESIGN

DEBORAH
PINALS
ASSOCIATE
1201
WEST
PEACHTREE
STREET
SUITE 3630
ATLANTA, GA
30309
404 873 AVID
404 320 1737

167

MICHAEL BONILLA
ILLUSTRATION

4743 Shaunee Creek
Dayton, Ohio 45415
513-275-7071
513-274-5591 Fax

MICHAEL BONILLA
ILLUSTRATION

4743 Shaunee Creek
Dayton, Ohio 45415
513-275-7071
513-274-5591 Fax

4743 Shaunee Creek
Dayton, Ohio 45415

MICHAEL BONILLA
ILLUSTRATION

Michael Bonilla (Illustrator)

The stationery system for a freelance illustrator starting his own studio features candid little elements of his technique.

DESIGN FIRM:

Graphica, Inc., Miamisburg, Ohio

ART DIRECTOR/

DESIGNER:

Drew Cronenwett

ILLUSTRATOR:

Michael Bonilla

BUDGET: Design: pro bono; printing: $1500

PRINTING PROCESS:

3 flat colors, offset

CUSTOM TEXTILES

SUSAN FOREMAN

Post Office Box 1044, Woodstock, Georgia 30188-1044
Telephone 404.591.2204 Facsimile 404.516.7136

Post Office Box 1044
Woodstock, Georgia 30188-1044

Post Office Box 1044, Woodstock, Georgia 30188-1044 Telephone 404.591.2204 Facsimile 404.516.7136

Custom Textiles, Inc.

Post Office Box 671061
Marietta, Georgia 30066

The yarn image indicates that this specialized textile firm creates custom fabrics to particular specifications and needs. The identity is carried through on fabric swatch cards, notebook covers, notepads, and other marketing tools.

DESIGN FIRM: Patti Ratcliffe Graphic Design, Charlotte, North Carolina

DESIGNER: Patti Ratcliffe

PRINTING PROCESS: 4-color PMS match, a different color of yarn on each piece

169

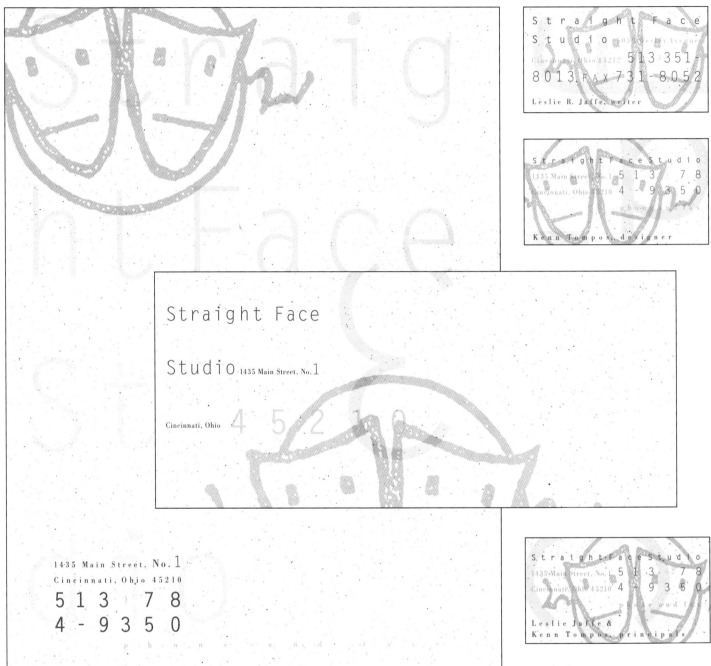

Straight Face Studio 1435 Main Street, No. 1 Cincinnati, Ohio 45210

513 78 4 - 9 3 5 0

Four different cards were printed—two versions of a card with both partners' names and one each for individual partners. The same elements are in various locations on all cards and each card has one letter of the word "face."

DESIGN FIRM: Straight Face Studio, Cincinnati, Ohio

ART DIRECTOR: Kenn Tompos, Leslie Jaffe

DESIGNER: Kenn Tompos

BUDGET: Printing: $1300

PRINTING PROCESS: 3 match colors, offset lithography

The theme of the stationery was Sandra Frank's skill in photographing a variety of subjects: people/portraits, landscape/environmental, architecture, and still life/studio. The four-subject theme continues throughout the package with particular emphasis on the variations of her business card. Special care

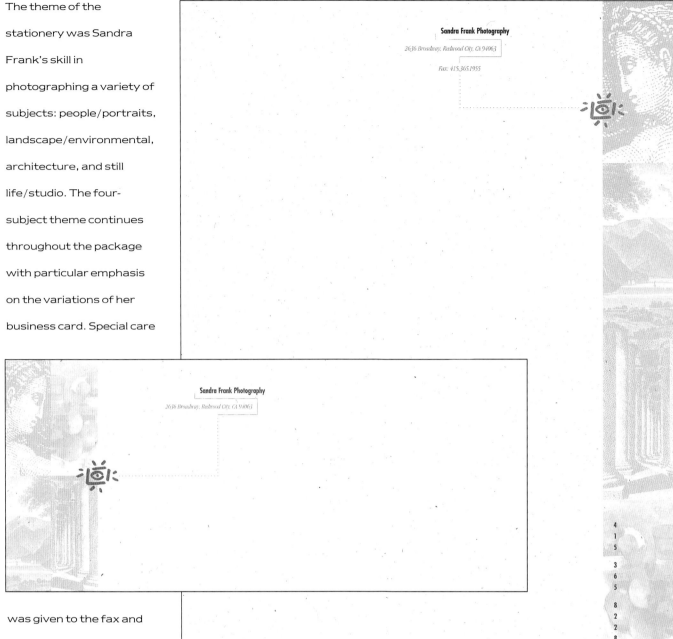

was given to the fax and photocopy factor of each image to insure readability.

DESIGN FIRM: Chikamura Design, San Francisco, California

ART DIRECTOR: Michael Chikamura

DESIGNERS: Lai-Kit Chan, Michael Chikamura, Glenn Randle

PRINTER: R.W. Nielsen Associates

BUDGET: Design: $1200; printing: $1200–$1500

PRINTING PROCESS: 3 match PMS colors, offset lithography

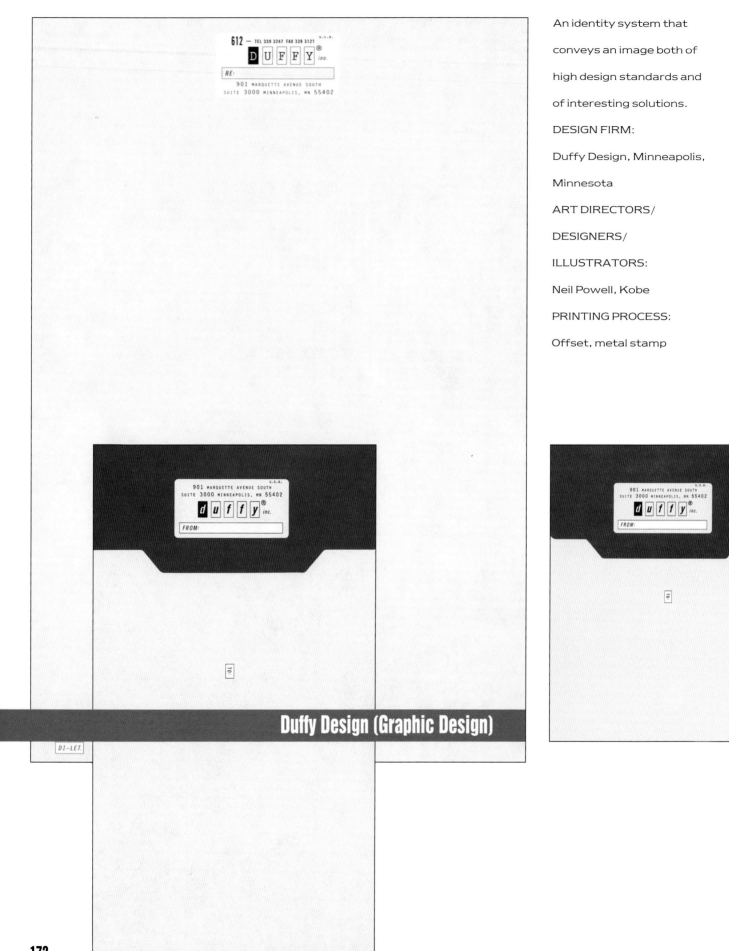

An identity system that conveys an image both of high design standards and of interesting solutions.

DESIGN FIRM:

Duffy Design, Minneapolis, Minnesota

ART DIRECTORS/

DESIGNERS/

ILLUSTRATORS:

Neil Powell, Kobe

PRINTING PROCESS:

Offset, metal stamp

Duffy Design (Graphic Design)

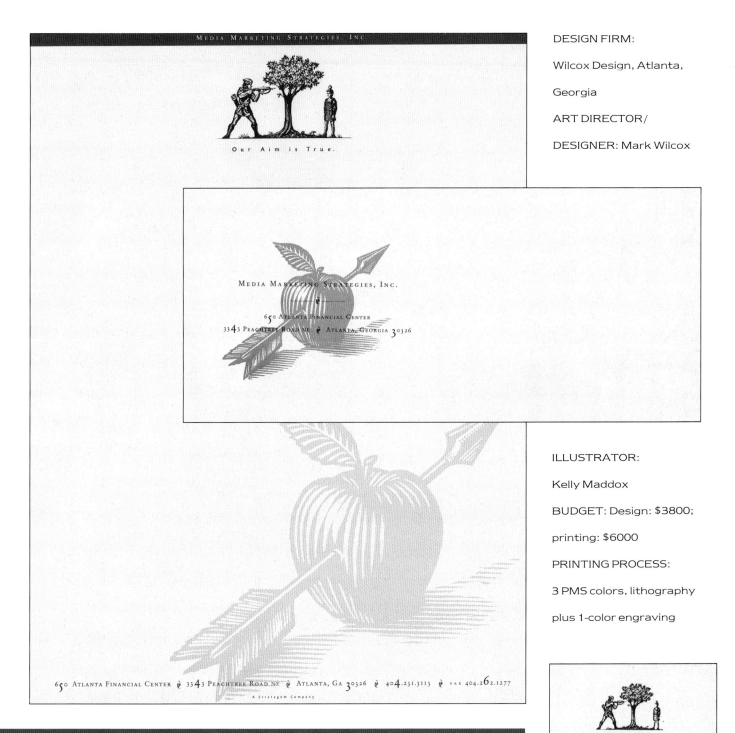

MEDIA MARKETING STRATEGIES, INC.

Our Aim is True.

MEDIA MARKETING STRATEGIES, INC.

650 ATLANTA FINANCIAL CENTER
3343 PEACHTREE ROAD NE ❦ ATLANTA, GEORGIA 30326

DESIGN FIRM:

Wilcox Design, Atlanta,

Georgia

ART DIRECTOR/

DESIGNER: Mark Wilcox

ILLUSTRATOR:

Kelly Maddox

BUDGET: Design: $3800;

printing: $6000

PRINTING PROCESS:

3 PMS colors, lithography

plus 1-color engraving

650 ATLANTA FINANCIAL CENTER ❦ 3343 PEACHTREE ROAD NE ❦ ATLANTA, GA 30326 ❦ 404.231.3113 ❦ FAX 404.262.1277

A Stratagem Company

Media Marketing Strategies, Inc. (Design/Marketing)

J U S T   W R I T E
Literary and Editorial Services

1160 TOPPER LANE
EL CAJON, CALIFORNIA 92021
619 596 0312 • 619 236 8578

J U S T   W R I T E
№ 1 · EXTRA SHARP
Literary and Editorial Services

SERVICES	HOURLY RATES
PROOFREADING	$20

- Correct typographical errors
- Note poor type quality
- Conform manuscript to type specifications

LIGHT COPYEDITING	$25

- Correct spelling, punctuation, grammar, and usage errors
- Conform manuscript to established style (capitalization, spacing, abbreviation, etc.)

MEDIUM COPYEDITING	$30

Same as light copyediting, plus:

- Tighten sloppy or wordy writing
- Eliminate sexism, racism and stereotyping (if requested)
- Note flaws in logic
- Cross-check bibliographic references and footnotes

HEAVY COPYEDITING	$45

Same as medium copyediting, plus:

- Rewrite unclear text
- Change passive to active voice
- Note potentially libelous passages, factual inaccuracies, or other legal liabilities
- Eliminate jargon
- Make suggestions to author for cuts, additions, and rearrangements

SUBSTANTIVE EDITING	$50

- Assess for style, tone, structure, logic, and accuracy
- Reorganize manuscript
- Rewrite text
- Eliminate wordiness
- Write transitions and summaries
- Consult with author to resolve inconsistencies and clarify confusing passages

DEVELOPMENTAL EDITING/COLLABORATION	*

- Develop manuscript with author
- Help shape manuscript from outlines, drafts, notes, or transcripts
- Make recommendations as to form, style, and sequence
- Provide feedback, guidance, encouragement, and constructive criticism

COPYWRITING/SCRIPTWRITING	*

- Write or develop marketing and presentation copy or audiotape/videotape scripts

PROJECT MANAGEMENT	*

- Coordinate production with publisher and/or author
- Hire/manage subcontracted labor
- Secure permissions and copyright

INDEXING	$20
RESEARCHING/SUMMARIZING	$35

* Fees vary depending on complexity of project and intended usage.

A graphic identity for a new business targeted primarily to nonfiction authors and publishers.

DESIGN FIRM: Robert Mott & Associates, San Diego, California

ART DIRECTOR/ DESIGNER: Robert Mott

PHOTOGRAPHER: Glenn Steiner

BUDGET: Client partner married to designer; photography donated; film donated; printing: around $1000 (cost)

PRINTING PROCESS: 2-color

Kevin O. Mooney Photography (Advertising/Editorial Photography)

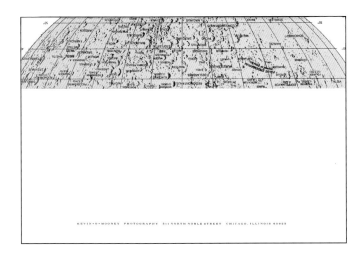

Stationery package clearly defines an identity to separate this Mooney from another photographer with the same name.

DESIGN FIRM:
Design Kitchen, Chicago, Illinois

DESIGNER: Janice Clark
BUDGET: Printing: $3000
PRINTING PROCESS:
5-color (yellow, green, blue, purple, black), offset

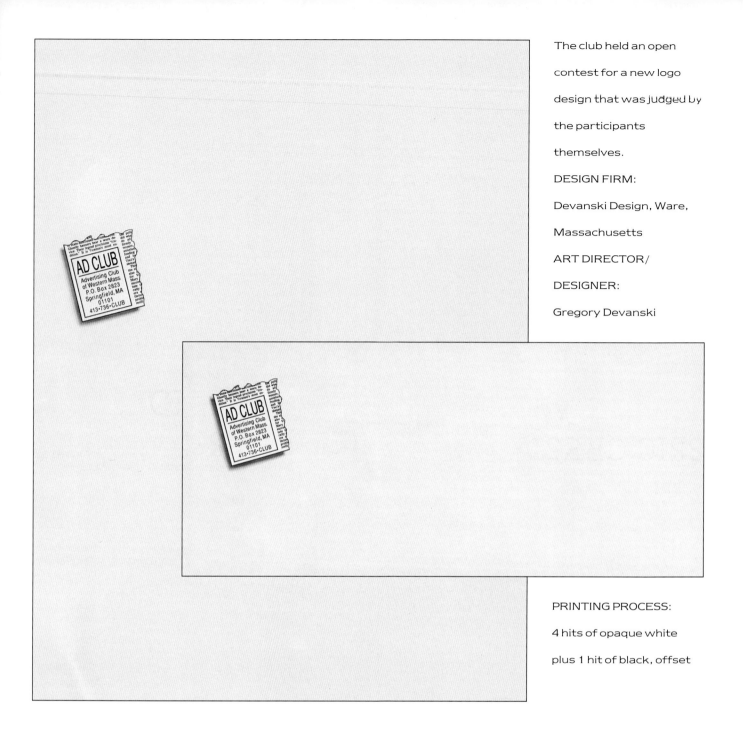

The club held an open contest for a new logo design that was judged by the participants themselves.

DESIGN FIRM:

Devanski Design, Ware, Massachusetts

ART DIRECTOR/

DESIGNER:

Gregory Devanski

PRINTING PROCESS:

4 hits of opaque white

plus 1 hit of black, offset

Advertising Club of Western Massachusetts

HOOSIER
WINDOWS

P.O. Box 768   Fort Wayne, IN 46801-0768   219-422-2225   800-344-4849   FAX 219-422-2538

St. James Collection

Hoosier Windows (Replacement Windows)

HOOSIER
WINDOWS

John Ackerman
President

HOOSIER
WINDOWS

P.O. Box 768   219-422-2225
Ft. Wayne, IN 46801-0768   800-344-4849
                        FAX 219-422-2538

St. James Collection

The fact that 87% of

Hoosier window sales are

in double hungs dictated

the logo: the two panes of

glass in the double-hung

window represent the *H* in

Hoosier.

DESIGN FIRM:

RileySimmons, Inc.,

Fort Wayne, Indiana

ART DIRECTOR:

Audrey Riley

DESIGNERS: Audrey Riley,

Bob Kiel

PHOTOGRAPHER:

Jim Miller

BUDGET: Design: $637;

printing: $1365

PRINTING PROCESS:

4-color, offset

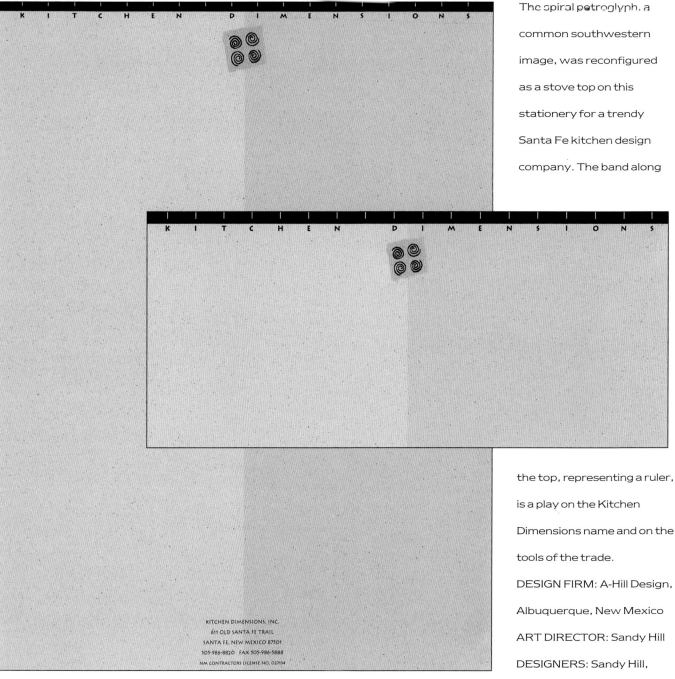

The spiral petroglyph, a common southwestern image, was reconfigured as a stove top on this stationery for a trendy Santa Fe kitchen design company. The band along the top, representing a ruler, is a play on the Kitchen Dimensions name and on the tools of the trade.

DESIGN FIRM: A-Hill Design, Albuquerque, New Mexico

ART DIRECTOR: Sandy Hill

DESIGNERS: Sandy Hill, Tom Antreasian

PRINTING: Century Graphics

BUDGET: Design of logo and letterhead package: $2500; printing: $1200

PRINTING PROCESS: 2-color plus embossing

The promotional program for the grand opening of this church in Boise, Idaho, was designed to express the idea of "church" in a fresh new way.

DESIGN FIRM:

Kerr & Company Design, Vancouver, British Colombia

DESIGNER/ILLUSTRATOR:

David Kerr

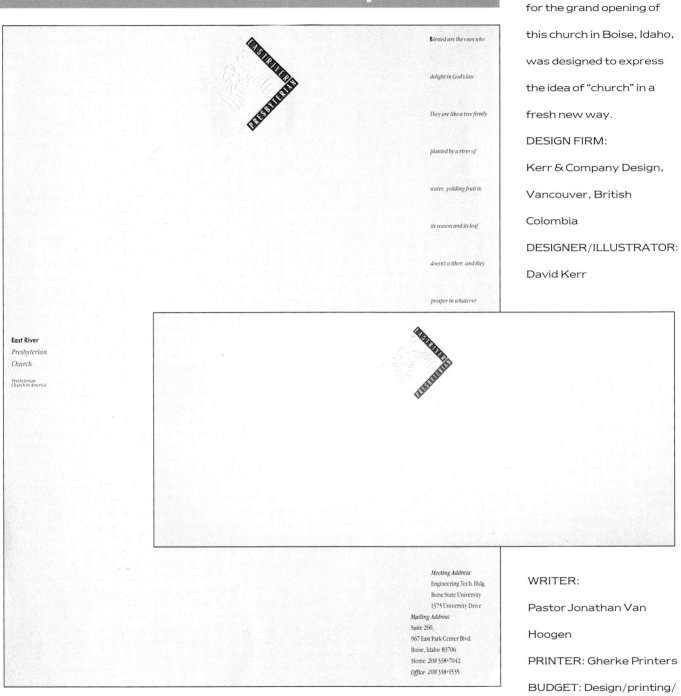

Blessed are the ones who

delight in God's law:

They are like a tree firmly

planted by a river of

water, yeilding fruit in

its season and its leaf

doesn't wither, and they

prosper in whatever

East River
Presbyterian
Church

Presbyterian
Church in America

Meeting Address:
Engineering Tech. Bldg.
Boise State University
1375 University Drive
Mailing Address:
Suite 260,
967 East Park Center Blvd.
Boise, Idaho 83706
Home *208 338·7042*
Office 208 338·1535

East River
Presbyterian
Church   **Jonathan Van Hoogen**
Pastor B.A., M.Div.

Meeting Address:
Engineering Tech. Bldg.
Boise State University
1375 University Drive
Mailing Address:
Suite 260,
967 East Park Center Blvd.
Boise, Idaho 83706
Presbyterian   Home *208 338·7042*
Church in   *Office 208 338·1535*
America

WRITER:

Pastor Jonathan Van Hoogen

PRINTER: Gherke Printers

BUDGET: Design/printing/ embossing: $3500

PRINTING PROCESS:

2-color, dull thermography plus embossed illustration

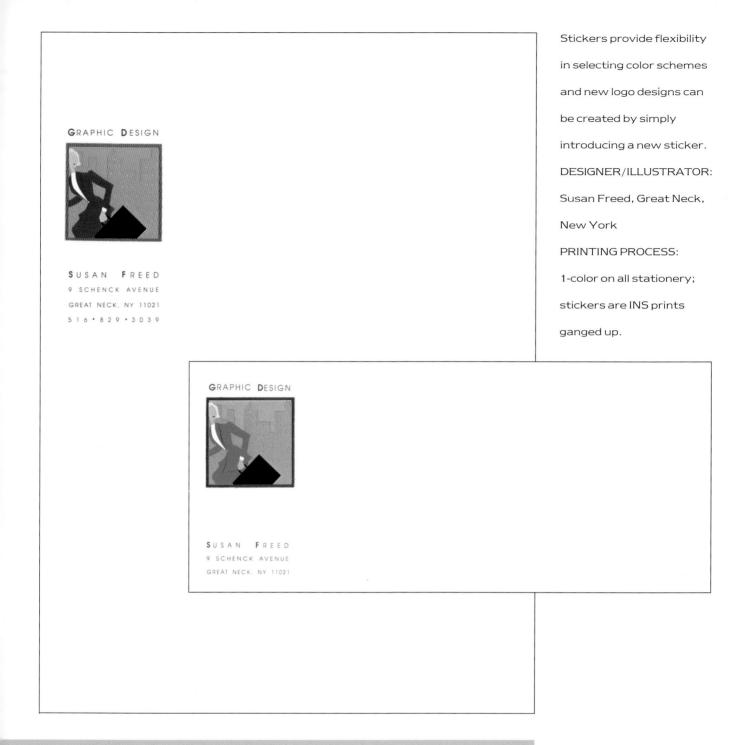

Stickers provide flexibility in selecting color schemes and new logo designs can be created by simply introducing a new sticker.

DESIGNER/ILLUSTRATOR: Susan Freed, Great Neck, New York

PRINTING PROCESS: 1-color on all stationery; stickers are INS prints ganged up.

Susan Freed (Graphic Designer)

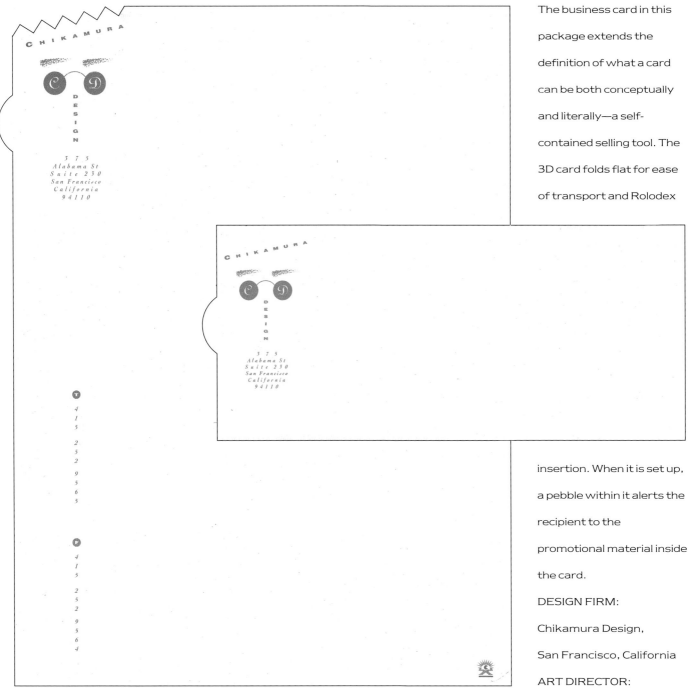

The business card in this package extends the definition of what a card can be both conceptually and literally—a self-contained selling tool. The 3D card folds flat for ease of transport and Rolodex insertion. When it is set up, a pebble within it alerts the recipient to the promotional material inside the card.

DESIGN FIRM:
Chikamura Design,
San Francisco, California
ART DIRECTOR:
Michael Chikamura
DESIGNERS:
Michael Chikamura, Lai-Kit
Chan, Andrew Fukutome
PRINTER: R.W. Nielsen
Associates
BUDGET: Printing: $2500
PRINTING PROCESS:
2 match PMS colors, offset
lithography, diecutting

Chikamura Design (Graphic Design)

Other Contributors